WARRIOR • 154

BORDER REIVER 1513–1603

KEITH DURHAM

ILLUSTRATED BY G & S EMBLETON

Series editor Marcus Cowper

First published in Great Britain in 2011 by Osprey Publishing
Midland House, West Way, Botley, Oxford OX2 0PH, UK
44-02 23rd St, Suite 219, Long Island City, NY 11101, USA
E-mail: info@ospreypublishing.com

A CIP catalogue record for this book is available from the British Library.

ISBN: 978 1 84908 1 931

E-book ISBN: 978 1 84908 194 8

Editorial by Ilios Publishing Ltd, Oxford, UK (www.iliospublishing.com)
Page layout by: Mark Holt
Index by Mike Parkin
Typeset in Sabon and Myriad Pro
Originated by PPS Grasmere Ltd
Printed in China through Worldprint Ltd

11 12 13 14 15 10 9 8 7 6 5 4 3 2 1

www.ospreypublishing.com

ACKNOWLEDGEMENTS

I would like to thank the following for their help and kindness:
'The Borderers', particularly Jeffrey and Janet Burn and Sean Barbour.
From 'The Best of Times, the Worst of Times', Martin Francis, Flora Fairbairn
and Andrew Dineley. At the Royal Armouries, Leeds, Stuart Ivinson,
and from 'The Old Gaol', Hexham, Janet Goodridge. My thanks also go
to Phil Smith at Osprey, the illustrator David Simon and to Gerry Embleton
for producing such a fine set of colour plates. Last but not least, to
Ruth Scott for skilfully navigating the 'wastes and crooked passes'
of the Border Marches. Unless otherwise indicated all the images
are from the author's collection.

ARTIST'S NOTE

Readers may care to note that the original paintings from which
the colour plates in this book were prepared are available for private sale.
All reproduction copyright whatsoever is retained by the Publishers.
All enquiries should be addressed to:

www.gerryembleton.com

The Publishers regret that they can enter into no correspondence upon
this matter.

THE WOODLAND TRUST

Osprey Publishing are supporting the Woodland Trust, the UK's leading
woodland conservation charity, by funding the dedication of trees.

CONTENTS

BORDER REIVER 1513–1603

INTRODUCTION

In 1649, William Gray, in his *Chorographia*, presented us with this concise and accurate history of the English Border Marches:

The noblemen and gentry of the north, hath been always imployed in their native country, in the warres of the Kings of England, against the Scots; all of them holding their lands in knights service, to attend the warres in their own persons, with horse and speare, as the manner of fighting was in those days. Some gentlemen held their land in cornage by blowing a horne, to give notice that the Scots, their enemies had invaded the land. The Scots, their neighbouring enemies, hath made the inhabitants of Northumberland fierce and hardy, while sometimes they kept themselves exercised in the warres, being a most warre-like nation, and excellent good light-horsemen, wholly addicting themselves to wars and armes, not a gentleman amongst them that hath not his castle or tower. It was the policy of the Kings of England, to cherish and maintain martiall prowess among them in the marches of the kingdom. There was lord wardens of the east, west and middle marches appointed, who had the power by martiall law to repress all enormities and outrages committed in the Borders. They had their laws, called Border laws.

Gray continues:

There is many dales, the chief are Tinedale and Reedsdale, a countrey that William the Conqueror did not subdue, retaining to this day ancient laws and customs... whereby the lands of the father is equally divided at his death amongst all his sonnes [a custom known as 'gavelkind']. These Highlanders are famous for theeving; they are all bred up and live by theft. They come down from these dales into the low countries, and carry away horses and cattell so cunningly, that it will be hard for any to get them or their cattell, except they be acquainted with some master thiefe, who for some mony (which they call saufey-mony) may help them to [retrieve] their stoln goods – or deceive them. There is many every yeare brought in of them into the gaole of Newcastle, and at the assizes, are condemned and hanged, sometimes twenty or thirty… the people of this country hath one barbarous custome amongst them; if any two be displeased, they expect no law, but bang it out breavely, one and his kindred against the other and his: they will subject themselves to no justice, but in an inhuman and barbarous manner fight and kill one another: they run together in clangs as they terme it or names. This fighting they call their feides [feuds], or deadly feides.

Gray's observations touch upon many of the key factors that gave rise to a frontier community that, by the beginning of the 16th century, was deeply immersed in an archaic culture of warfare and lawlessness.

For most of the 13th century, the people of the Anglo-Scottish Borderland, having much in common, coexisted peacefully and enjoyed many years of stability and prosperity. This happy state of affairs was soon to be shattered by the aggressive English monarch Edward I, whose ambitions included the total annexation of the kingdom of Scotland. In 1296, having become frustrated by his lack of progress, he unleashed his army in a series of vicious invasions into the Scottish Lowlands. The Scots hit back and for the next 300 years the Borderland was racked by bouts of open hostility between the two kingdoms and frequently stripped bare by the plundering armies of both nations. Amongst numerous battles and skirmishes, the Scots scored victories at Stirling Bridge in 1297 and at Bannockburn in 1314, where Scotland finally won its independence under Robert the Bruce. In 1402, however, the English

The Cheviot Hills form a natural barrier between the two kingdoms and proved an effective deterrent to invading armies, which invariably passed through the East and West Marches. These remote hills are characterized by their bare, rounded summits and twisting, steep-sided valleys, as can be seen in this view of Rowhope and Trows in Upper Coquetdale, Northumberland. Using intimate knowledge of this wild and disorientating landscape, raiders were able to pass undetected from one realm into the other.

In three centuries of Border warfare, these flat salt marshes at Burgh-by-Sands on the Solway Firth were frequently crossed by the invading armies of both nations. The memorial commemorates the passing of Edward I, 'Hammer of the Scots', who died here of dysentery in 1307. The warlike monarch left strict instructions to his son, 'never to make peace with Scotland until the nation was subdued'.

At the battle of Flodden Field in 1513, Scots Borderers under the command of Lord Hume acquitted themselves well in the early stages of the battle, as did their English counterparts under Lord Dacre. However, as the battle progressed, the Borderers of both nations disengaged from the conflict, thus avoiding the ensuing bloodbath in which James IV, the flower of his nobility and 10,000 of his soldiers met their deaths. (Rick Scollins)

were victorious at Homildon Hill and, in 1482, seized and secured the important bridgehead of Berwick-upon-Tweed. Hostilities between the two nations continued and in 1513, at the greatest of all border battles, the Scots under James IV were heavily defeated with great loss of life at Flodden Field in Northumberland.

As a consequence, during this bitter war of attrition the Borderland became a buffer zone between the two kingdoms and each government offered its subjects land and low-rent tenancies in return for military service as and when required. In addition, as a way of fomenting strife in the opposite kingdom, Borderers were actively encouraged to make raids on their erstwhile neighbours across the 'line', burning their homes, rustling their livestock and leaving a trail of death and destruction in their wake. Raid begat raid and, by the beginning of the 16th century, for a great many Borderers 'reiving' had become an accepted way of life. Consequently, even during periods when peace reigned between the two countries, there was little respite for honest Border folk who were forever plagued by incessant raids, murder, theft and arson. This in turn led to deadly feuds erupting between many of the great Border families and also gave rise to a web of extortion involving crippling payments of 'blackmail' – all of which 'utterly beggared' the region.

In the 16th century, John Leslie, Bishop of Ross, who seems to have been well acquainted with the Borderers and their customs, sympathized with their predicament, acknowledging in his *History of Scotland* that 'in time of war, they are readily reduced to extreme poverty by the almost daily inroads of the enemy, so, on the restoration of peace, they entirely neglect to cultivate their lands, though fertile, from fear of the fruits of their labour being immediately destroyed by a new war... whence it happens that they seek their subsistence by robberies, or rather by plundering and rapine.'

Both nations, however, realized that their intermittent warring, combined with the political hostility that existed between them, had created in the Borderlands a lawless and dangerous society. In an attempt to bring some stability to the region, the two governments, in an agreement known as the Law of the Marches, divided their territories into East, West and Middle Marches and men of esteem from each realm were appointed as Wardens to govern them in matters both military and judicial. On the English side of the line, March Wardens were invariably drawn from the southern shires, thus ensuring they owed no allegiance to any of the Border 'graynes' (families) with whom they would be dealing, whilst on the Scottish side Wardens were traditionally appointed from the local gentry. It therefore comes as no surprise to discover that when cross-Border disputes arose, Scottish Wardens were frequently accused of favouring their kinsmen and followers.

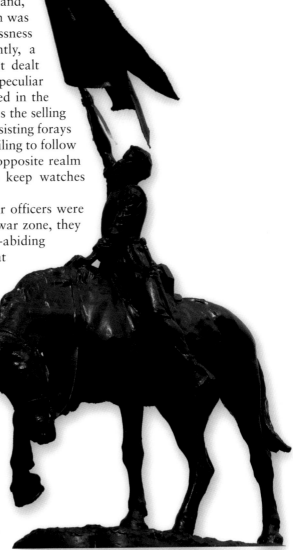

In spite of Scotland's crushing defeat at Flodden Field in 1513, Scots Borderers could still pack a punch. This monument commemorates the return of the young men of Hawick after a skirmish in 1514 at Hornshole, where they routed a party of English marauders and captured the Bishop of Hexham's flag. The statue was sculpted by Major William Beattie MC, RFA, who was killed in action in France, 1918.

Usually underpaid and often overworked, it was the Warden's unenviable task to impose the rule of law and order on the devious inhabitants within his March, but trying to keep such unruly people in check was no easy task. Whilst the basic laws of the land may have been adequate enough elsewhere in England and Scotland, both governments realized that additional legislation was required to deal with the unique brand of lawlessness that flourished along the Borderline. Consequently, a supplementary code of justice was drawn up that dealt specifically with those criminal activities that were peculiar to the region. This legislation, which was enshrined in the Border Laws, dealt with such treasonable offences as the selling of weapons, armour and horses across the Border, assisting forays from the opposite realm into one's own kingdom, failing to follow the 'fray', intermarrying with a woman from the opposite realm without the Warden's permission and failing to keep watches appointed for the defence of the country.

However, because the March Wardens and their officers were operating in what was essentially a bandit-ridden war zone, they often proved ineffective in protecting the law-abiding Borderer and his family from the sudden violence that could descend upon them. Consequently, on both sides of the Border, people of all social classes lived in constant fear of their lives and for security they banded together in their own 'graynes' to whom they gave a loyalty that transcended any national allegiance. Living in a network of small castles, fortified tower houses, defensible farm houses known as 'bastles' and robust turf-and-timber strongholds called 'peles', the Borderer came to rely on his kinsmen in times of trouble. If he was 'spoyled' or 'bereaved' by raiders and sought redress by lawful means, he was well aware that securing any kind of satisfaction from his tormentors could often prove to be a futile and dangerous enterprise. And so, with his friends and kinsmen, he too rode with the moonlight and, with 'lance and steel bonnet', engaged in the nightly mayhem that 'shook loose the Border'.

CHRONOLOGY

1509	Henry VIII becomes King of England.
1513	The battle of Flodden Field; the Scots suffer a devastating defeat with the loss of their king, James IV, and many of his nobles.
1530	King James V purges the Scottish Borders and executes the notorious reiver Johnnie Armstrong.
1542	The battle of Solway Moss; an invading Scottish army 16,000 strong is ignominiously routed on the river Esk by a considerably smaller force of English Border 'prickers'.
1544	The beginning of a series of English campaigns in the Scottish Lowlands that became known as the 'rough wooing'.
1545	The battle of Ancrum Moor; an English force under Sir Ralph Eure and Sir Brian Laiton is heavily defeated by the Scots.
1547	The battle of Pinkie Cleugh; the Scots are roundly defeated by an English force under the command of the Duke of Somerset; Henry VIII dies.
1548	French reinforcements arrive in Scotland under the command of the Sieur d'Esse; Mary, Queen of Scots, is sent to safety in France and betrothed to the dauphin, Francis.
1549	The recapture of Ferniehirst Castle; the 'rough wooing' effectively comes to an end.
1558	Elizabeth I ascends the English throne.
1561	Mary, Queen of Scots, returns from France to Scottish soil.
1566	The Earl of Bothwell is badly wounded by Little Jock Elliot.
1567	Bothwell marries Mary, Queen of Scots.
1575	The Raid of the Redeswire; a truce day degenerates into a large-scale fracas, with loss of life to both Scots and English Borderers.
1587	The execution of Mary, Queen of Scots.
1596	The execution of Geordie Burn by Sir Robert Carey; the rescue of Kinmont Willie Armstrong from Carlisle Castle by Sir Walter Scott of Buccleuch.
1598	Sir Robert Carey becomes Warden of the English Middle March.

1601	Carey launches an offensive against the Armstrongs of Liddesdale.
1603	The death of Elizabeth I; James VI of Scotland is proclaimed James I of England and begins the pacification of the Borders.

LIFE ON THE BORDER MARCHES

In the mid-16th century, Sir Robert Bowes, a 'most expert Borderer' who served as Warden of the English Middle and East Marches, paints this vivid picture of a thriving criminal society and, although he is writing about Tynedale and Redesdale, his comments could equally be applied across the Border region. Noting that although there was apparently much arable and pasture land, he points out that 'the country is much overpopulated and not cultivated at all, whereby the young and active people, for lack of living, be constrained to steal or spoil continually, either in England or Scotland, for maintaining of their lives'. He continues:

> Of every surname there be sundry families or graynes, as they call them, of which there be certain headsmen that leadeth and answereth for all the rest. And do lay pledges for them when need requireth, and there be some among them that have never stolen themselves, which they call 'true men'. And yet such will have rascals to steal for them, either on horseback or on foot, whom they do reset [harbour or protect] or at least receive part of the stolen goods; or at least make all the means they may for the deliverance of such thieves. If any of them chance to be taken, either by… the party that owned the stolen goods, whereby to stop his pursuit, or else to labour with the officers by all means that they can, to acquit and discharge such thieves from just correction.

Bowes concludes his observations with the following warning. 'If any true men of England get knowledge of the theft or thieves that steale his goods' and were reckless enough to 'pursue the extremity of the law against the thief', and 'the thief be of any great surname or kindred, and be lawfully executed by order of justice, the rest of his kin or surname bear as much malice, which they call deadly feud, against such as follow the law against their cousin the thief, as though he had unlawfully killed him with a sword.'

As mentioned by William Gray in his *Chorographia*, the local custom known as 'gavelkind', which caused widespread poverty and in turn led to theft, also impacted on the Borderer's ability to meet his military obligations to the Crown. Writing to William Cecil, Lord Burghley, in 1596, Ralph, 3rd Lord Eure, who served as Warden of the English Middle March from 1595 to 1598, observes that 'Tyndale has a custom, that on a farmer or owner's death, every man child has an equal part of the lease or land, whereby beggars increase and [military] service decays, for neither elder nor younger can keep horse – Redesdale claims the like.' Responding to these concerns, Burghley, the Lord Treasurer, agrees, noting that 'the inhabitants of Northumberland, Cumberland and Westmorland and the Bishopric who were formerly freed from subsidies… were bound to defend the frontier at their own charges, as also the inferior sort and tenants, who held on low rents… and ancient custom… are now decayed and unable for this service'.

The Border Marches

Blaming unscrupulous landlords for this lamentable state of affairs he berates them 'for laying down their lands in pasture in large farms... suppressing small holders, letting to the Scots' and impoverishing their tenants with 'heavy fines and greedy demands'.

Whatever the causes, the culture of criminality was deeply ingrained in Border society. Lord Scrope, Warden of the English West March, speaking of the powerful Grahams, touches on another curse which blighted the Border region: 'they are so strong by intermarriages in Scotland and England... that they are able to trouble the peace of both countries... few gentlemen can keep their goods safe unless matched with them, or have them as tenants, or pay blak mayle'. Many law-abiding Borderers lived under the shadow of blackmail, which was the levying of protection money by powerful families such as the Armstrongs and the Grahams. In 1595, Sir Robert Carey, an energetic Border officer of whom we shall hear more, informs us that even 'the chief [men] of the country, all but three or four, are driven to pay "blakemaelle"... to some Scots thief to save him from the rest. The poor and those unable to pay tribut to thos caterpilers are daily ridden upon and spoiled.'

It is also apparent that much of this endemic lawlessness involved Borderers plundering and harassing on their own side of the line, as witnessed in 1523 by the Bishop of Carlisle who wrote to Cardinal Wolsey, Henry VIII's Lord Chancellor, 'Ther is more thefte, more extorcyon by Englis theffs than

The Border Marches were infested with 'broken men' and 'clanless loons', being rascals at the bottom of the social ladder without a responsible headman or chief. They were held as outlaws who were 'any man's prey' and, like this well-armed group, rode together in ragged gangs, plundering, rustling and burning until their luck eventually ran out.

there is by all the Scotts of Scotland. Ther is noo man which is nott in a hold strong that hathe or maye have any cattell, that are moveable in suretie through the Bishopryke… all Northumberland likewise.' There was also much collusion between Scots and English Borderers, both on a social level and in their criminal enterprises. In his *Report on the Middle March* in 1595, Sir Robert Carey complains that 'tristing' (courting) between Scots and English 'without the warden's leave, which is March treason… is as common as our men meeting in the markets' and points out that most 'men of account… have Scotsmen dwelling in their houses, who are chief guides for the spoil of the poor'. That same year, Sir Ralph Eure reported that most of the misdemeanours he was forced to deal with 'were furthered by evil disposed English' joined in marriage 'with the clans and families of the Scots', adding that their 'constant incursions… have so weakened the people that they cannot keep horses as formerly and are forced to "trist" and combine with the outlaws'.

This well-preserved 16th-century tower house, known as Hollows or Gilnockie, is an Armstrong stronghold standing above the river Esk near Canonbie in Dumfries and Galloway. Note the narrow windows, shot holes and on the crow-stepped gable, the stone beacon which would be fired up on the approach of raiders.

The habitual destruction wrought by these cross-border confederacies was astounding. Earlier in the century, on 16 May 1525, Sir William Bulmer and Sir William Eure, in an attempt to combat such lawlessness and reinforce their authority in the unruly district of Tynedale, tried to persuade Cardinal Wolsey to retain garrisons at Tarsett Hall, Chipchase Castle and Hesleyside and warned of the consequences if they were disbanded. 'The Armystronges of Liddersdaill and the thieffs of Ewysdaill, [are] joined with the Kynge's rebelles of Tyndaill… and keepeth all company to gedders which is thowght shall make mony disspoilles of the Kynge's subjects, assoyn as the garrison shalbe discharged.' Shortly thereafter, in spite of the aforementioned garrisons being present, their fears were realized when '400 Scots, with the rebelles of Tynedale, came to Tarsett Hall and Hesleyside, where the Kynge's garrisons lay, and there took 55 horses and prisoners, and kylled and brount [burnt]. And on 13th June, came 600 Scotsmen, with the rebelles of Tendale, and took forty men and forty horses, and brount and kylled divers men.' Early the next month, the seemingly endless cycle of violence continued when Eure, accompanied by Sir Ralph Fenwick and a company of 'hayrcharys' (archers) and 'fyfte sperys', mounted a retaliatory raid against the 'rebelles' of Tynedale and having seized their goods and cattle, burnt their dwellings to the ground.

The mid-16th century also proved a particularly difficult time for the people of the Scottish Borders. During the period 1544–49, in addition to the usual raids and reprisals, the English launched a series of brutal incursions, some of which amounted to minor invasions that were deliberately intended to terrorize and cripple the Scottish Lowlands. These devastating raids were the final stages in Henry VIII's attempts to coerce Scottish factions that were reluctant to countenance the marriage of their infant Queen Mary to Henry's son, Edward, thus forging an alliance that would effectively allow Henry to seize control of Scotland.

Some idea of the damage inflicted on the Scottish Borders during this so-called 'rough wooing' is evident in the Earl of Hertford's report when he brought 'fyre and sword' to the Scottish Middle March in 1545. Cutting a broad swathe of misery through the countryside around Ferniehirst and Lanton, Hertford assured his king that in future, he will 'not need such great garrisons in the Borders', adding that 'within this iii [three] nights, Godde willing, Kelsey [Kelso]… shall be bront [burnt], with all the corn in the said town… and then they [the Scots] shall have noo place to lye any garyson in nygh unto the Borders.' The previous year, Sir Thomas Wharton had laid claim to the destruction of 124 Scottish 'townes, graneries, hamlettes' and 'brought away 285 oxen and kine, 332 horses and nags, 4,710 sheep and goats, 408 prisoners, and slew 38 Scotsmen'.

Although many Scots Borderers remained defiant, others succumbed and, in order to secure protection from these English depredations, became 'assured' men. This involved lending their support to the English enterprise, promising to 'serve faithfully the King of England and all his Officers', to not 'attempt any displeasure on [the English] realme' and to desist from challenging English raids into Scotland. Some Scots Borderers, however, saw distinct advantages in the union with England and with an eye to extending their own holdings and settling some old scores they willingly sided with the English and turned on those of their own countrymen who remained loyal to the Scottish cause. (In the eyes of the Scottish government 'assurance' was a treasonable offence and many of those who collaborated with the English were subsequently outlawed and lost their possessions.)

Standing near the Tarset Burn, Northumberland, is Black Middens, a late 16th-century 'bastle'. Erected by a wealthy farmer for security against raiders, this two-storey, defensible farmhouse was immensely strong for its relatively small size. Livestock could be secured in the basement, whilst the upper floor, which provided accommodation, would have been reached by means of a retractable ladder. The stone steps and ground-level doorway were added for convenience in more settled times.

In 1540, it was observed that 'the people of the borders towards England lyveth in much povertie and penurye, hauving no howses but such as a man may buylde within iii or iiii howres'. Such dwellings would have been small and crudely constructed from mud and timber, whilst this timber and turf house, which incorporates a lower course of stone, is obviously the property of a wealthier man. (Courtesy of the Historic Hexham Trust)

English garrisons became established at key points in the Scottish Lowlands and in response the Scots invoked the 'Auld Alliance' and enlisted help from their French allies. In 1548, a force of about 12,000 professional soldiers under the command of Andre of Montalembert, Sieur d'Esse, landed in support of the Scots cause and, soon after their arrival, Jean de Beaugue, an officer who accompanied d'Esse, observed:

> To what a low Ebb of Fortune the Scots were at this time reduc'd when the Enemy, after having Burnt their Towns, Ravag'd the whole Low Country, and Usurp'd the greatest Strengths of their Frontiers, kept them closely pent up, that they durst not go abroad but in very considerable Numbers; and even then were so indifferently look'd upon by the English (a People always tainted with that Heresie, which imposes upon them a false Belief of their own Merit, beyond that of all Nations of the World) that about 500 Horse (for they had no more then in Scotland) durst scour the Fields both in Night-time and in broad Day, to the very Gates of the Capital, thunder in Arms over all that Sea-coast and incessantly plunder and harass the whole Neighbourhood.

It is plain to de Beague, however, that many of the Scots' troubles could be ascribed to their own 'feuds and Animosities at Home... so heartily did they distrust one another, that they... gave their Enemy an easy Opportunity of gaining the Ascendant over them'.

In addition to the ever present threat of violence under which Borderers lived, the disastrous effect that these campaigns could have on their daily existence cannot be overestimated. In 1549, de Beague reports that 'when [our] army was force'd to ly at Jedburgh', soldiers who were 'in Want of all Necessaries... to preserve their lives', scavenged the surrounding countryside and many took to 'Hunting and Fishing' but adds, 'the Scots assure me' that in doing so 'they destroy'd the very Brood of the Fishes of Ged [a river that gives its name to Jedburgh] and that none have been seen in it since that time'. At first glance, this would seem a minor complaint amidst the greater atrocities that were being inflicted on the Scottish Lowlands at this time, but the total depletion of fish stocks (and wildlife) would have impacted drastically on the local community, its economy and subsequent well being. The consequences must have been felt for a generation.

CRIME AND RETRIBUTION

'The Great Theeves'

Reiving was carried out by men from all levels of Border society and in spite of the efforts of the March Wardens and their officers to stop them, this criminal fraternity seem to have done rather well out of it. In 1597, Sir Robert Bowes reported that over the previous ten years, the 'value of the spoils by the Scots in these three Marches… amounts to £10,458.17s.8d in the East, £28,098.8s.5d in the Middle, and £54,422 in the West Marches' in all, a total of almost £93,000.00. (In 2009, an equivalent sum would be somewhere in the region of £20,925,000.00). Even allowing for some degree of exaggeration, reiving was indeed a lucrative business! Although most of those involved in this perilous activity came and went anonymously, the exploits of a few have been reliably recorded and what follows are brief accounts of some of the more notable players from the wrong side of the law.

In 1523 the Bishop of Carlisle wrote to Cardinal Wolsey, 'Exhamshire which loongeth [belongeth] to your Grace [is] worste of all, for in Exham selfe every markett day ther is four score or a hundred strong theffs, and the poore men and gentilmen also seethe them whiche did robbe them and ther goddys [goods] and dare nother complain of them by name, nor saye one word to them.' (Illustration by Angus McBride, courtesy of The Historic Hexham Trust)

 A

BLACKMAIL, 1596

In 1596, Lord Scrope wrote to the Privy Council berating the Grahams for

> their devilish devices… and awfulness to their neighbours. [Many of the tenants of Lanercost and Gilsland] to the number of thrie score or above… have paid blackmail to William Hayer [Haire] servant to Richard Grame and one Thomas Hetherington… called 'the merchant', demanding it for Grame's use [and] that the said William Hayer as Grame's special 'facturr', gave evil speeches and threatenings to the above [tenants] to make them pay, also to those who would not pay. With the exception of one 'Widow Smyth', who had paid blackmail, those tenants who had not paid blackmail had all their goods spoiled and carried off by the nephews and kinsmen of said Richard Grame, Scotsmen. These Scots kinsmen, before the robbery, inquired where the widow who had paid blackmail dwelt, and then harried all the rest, except her.

When one of the unfortunate tenants who had been 'spoiled' sought help from Thomas Carleton, Land Sergeant of Gilsland, he found the law officer socializing with none other than Richie Graham! In this scene, Thomas Hetherington reaches out to grasp the farmer's payment, while a well-armed William Haire looks on. Note the sturdy construction of the bastle house, the small windows and the ladder that allowed access to the doorway, which is situated well above ground level.

Johnnie Armstrong, Laird of Gilnockie or Hollows, was a notorious Scottish freebooter who intimidated great swathes of the English Borderland and extorted blackmail as far south as Newcastle-upon-Tyne. Tradition has it that he confined his depredations to the English side of the line and, based on that reason alone, many Scots have long regarded his betrayal and execution at the hands of James V as base treachery.

In 1528, it was reported that in times of trouble the fearsome Armstrong confederacy was able to muster 3,000 horsemen and shortly thereafter, they bragged that 'they would not be ordered by any king of Scots or England'. In the summer of 1530, in response to this increasing anarchy, the young King James V made plans to punish the chief malefactors of Liddesdale and Teviotdale, one of whom was 'John Armstrong, chief of one faction of the theives'. Armstrong's prestige, wealth and growing power was becoming a cause of increasing concern to the king and in addition, Armstrong's enemies had propagated a rumour that he 'had promised to bring that part of Scotland, for some miles, under the obedience of the English if he himself might be well considered for that service'. James accordingly issued a proclamation whereby the 'princepalls of all the surnames of the clannes on the borders' in the hope of securing a pardon for their sins 'wold cum in... and submit themselves [to] the king's will'. Accompanied by a great retinue of his nobles, His Highness duly rode through his Border Marches, dispensing justice and hunting as he went. On arriving at Carlenrig in Teviotdale, James invited Johnnie Armstrong to meet him. Gilnockie duly accepted the invitation and with his followers rode unarmed to meet his king. He and his men were immediately seized and executed without trial. Although the hanging of Johnnie and his companions at Carlenrig initially shook the Armstrongs, they soon recovered their strength and as we shall see, continued to be one of the most fearsome riding families on the frontier.

Operating on a somewhat smaller scale than Johnnie Armstrong was **Richie Graham**, a devious rogue, counterfeiter and great extortionist who controlled his criminal empire from his tower house at Brackenhill in the English West March. The Warden of the March, Lord Scrope, was continually tormented by the activities of the notorious Grahams, a surname 'very famous among the borderers for their martiall disposition' and in particular by Richie Graham of Brackenhill. Scrope's obsession in life was to 'bridle the insolencies of the Grames' and in 1596, he delights in having 'found proof that Richard Grame of Brakenhill, Will of the Rosetrees and Hutcheon Grame alias Richies Hutcheon, were all privie unto and complotters of the enterprise against this castell'. (At that time, Scrope was still smarting with embarrassment over Sir Walter Scott of Buccleuch's rescue of the notorious reiver Kinmont Willie Armstrong from Carlisle Castle, Scrope's own headquarters. As Scrope suspected, Richie Graham had almost certainly lent assistance to the 'enterprise'.) He continues, 'Brakenhill [also] stands indicted and outlawed for the murder of George Grame alias Percivalls Geordie; though he has agreed [settled] with the wife and young children... there are also charges of koyninge [counterfeiting], taking blackmail for protection of men and their goods [and] subordination or maintenance of theft and murders to be brought against him.' Scrope further reports that 'Brakenhill hath beggared the Queen's tenants of Whyte close near Leven, Richie, Clemy and Bartie Stories, and the rest there, who now pay no rent to the Queen, but to him, with black mail of 20s yearly... he hath [also] kept a "coyner" at work in the top of the tower of his own house and in Geordie Marks sheyld [a small building – in this case probably an outhouse] in the myllers howse end.'

The Grahams continued to flaunt Scrope's authority and Richie remained a constant thorn in his side. In July 1596, their feud further intensified when Scrope's officer Thomas Musgrave, Captain of Bewcastle, was engaged in a reprisal raid across the Border and having 'entered Scotland this night, and finding only empty houses, [he] returned homewards over carelessly, allowing his force to separate. Himself, with only ten men, fell into an ambush of the Scots near Bewcastle [and] was chased to the house of Brackenhill, where he hoped to take refuge, but those within shut the gates against him and [he] is taken prisoner to Scotland... such good services do the Grames to her

In this painting by the Border artist Tom Scott RSA, 'Auld Wat o' Harden' thunders forth on yet another foray into the English Marches. With numerous complaints lodged against him, Walter Scott of Harden was an inveterate raider and also played a leading role in the rescue of Kinmont Willie Armstrong from Carlisle Castle.

Majesty!' Although Scrope and his officers continued to pursue Richie, there is no record that justice ever caught up with him, which is hardly surprising, for it was common knowledge that anyone rash enough to offer evidence against Richie Graham could well end up 'stricken to the earth with the butt ende of Brakenhille's speare!'

Another of Scrope's sworn enemies was, of course, the formidable **William Armstrong** of Kinmont, a Falstaffian figure whose illegal arrest by Scrope's men on a truce day and subsequent rescue from Carlisle Castle in 1596, was celebrated in folklore and ballad. Married to an English Graham, he was deeply involved with the Maxwells, Wardens of the Scottish West March, and with a foot firmly planted in each kingdom, 'Kinmont Willie' pillaged extensively on both sides of the line. Riding from his tower at Morton Rigg, he led a number of large-scale, daylight forays into Tynedale in the early 1580s and in 1585 was carrying out raids on his own countrymen in Stirling. In 1593, accompanied by 'William Ellott of Lawreston, Martin Ellott of Bradley and the Laird of Mangerton... and 1,000 horsemen' he launched a massive raid into Tynedale, 'taking 1,005 head of nolt [cattle], 1,000 sheep and goats, 24 horses and meares... and taking insight [household goods] worth £300 sterling'. Often riding with such notables as Nebless Clem Croser, his reputation was such that in 1596, merchants in Edinburgh, on hearing rumours that he was coming to sack their town, hastily cleared their shops and booths of valuables and with great foreboding, prepared to defend themselves against the approaching spectre of 'Will Kinmonde, the common thieffe' and his gang of 'rank riders'. Following his rescue from Carlisle Castle, Willie was soon back in business, lifting livestock and ransoming prisoners, one of whom was the Captain of Bewcastle. In 1600, riding at the head of 140 freebooters who delighted in the name 'Sandy's Bairns', he plundered and burnt the village of Scotby and then finished off the day by rampaging around Carlisle, causing minor damage and generally making a nuisance of himself. The old reprobate was still active four years later and as far as we know, died peacefully of natural causes.

Further down the ladder in this criminal hierarchy was **Geordie Burn**, a common thug, hell raiser, murderer, womanizer and, inevitably, gallows bird. His career came to an abrupt end one dark night when he was caught in an ambush by troopers under Sir Robert Carey's command and taken with 'the bloody hand' whilst 'driving stolen cattle'. He was 'condemned by his own confession' and the night before the execution, Carey, who at that time was serving as Deputy Warden of the English East March, disguised himself as one of his own troopers and with two of his servants visited the condemned

THE CAPTURE OF GEORDIE BURN, 1596

On 14 September 1596, Sir Robert Carey reports the capture of Geordie Burn to Lord Burghley. 'This night being abroad with the xx [20] gaurrison men allowed me a watching, it was our good happe to mete with iiij [four] of the Burnes, the principallest theves of Tyvidale, with goodes dryving before theme which thei had stolen. Wee kild twoe of them forthright, tooke the third [Geordie Burn] sore wounded [about the head] before he would yeald, and the fowrth, the night being darck, unhappelye scapte away.' Geordie Burn wears a jack and unfortunately for him, has chosen not to wear his helmet that fateful night. He wields a wheel lock pistol, which once discharged, doubles as an axe. It follows an example in the Kelvingrove Museum, Glasgow. Carey's troopers are lightly clad, but well armed. The man on the left, who is attacking Burn, wears a combed burgonet and is armed with a sword and a wheel lock pistol, whilst the trooper in the foreground discharges his matchlock with devastating effect.

man in his cell. Chatting amiably with them, Geordie gave a frank and ultimately damning résumé of his misspent life: 'he voluntarily of himself said, that he had lived long enough to do so many villainies as he had done, and withal told us that he had lain with above forty men's wives, what in England, what in Scotland; and that he had killed seven Englishmen with his own hands, cruelly murdering them; that he had spent his whole life whoring, drinking, stealing and taking deep revenge for slight offences.' Having listened to the 'great spoylers' confession, Carey felt he could 'not have suffred so wicked a man to have lyved' and Geordie Burn was put to death at Berwick 'in the morning, very early' on 16 September 1596.

'Men of Esteem' – The March Wardens

Arrayed against these arrant lawbreakers were the March Wardens and their officers. On the English side of the line, between 1577 and 1594, the East March was governed by Lord Hundson, the Middle March came under Sir John Forster and the West March was controlled by Henry Lord Scrope who was succeeded by his son, Thomas. On the Scottish side, the Wardenship of the West March was usually held by a Maxwell; the Kerrs of Cessford and Ferniehirst by turns governed the Middle March; whilst on the East March the position was held by Lord Hume. Following Sir John Forster's ignominious dismissal in 1595, Ralph, 3rd Lord Eure took control of the English Middle March, but after three troubled years, resigned in 1598. He was succeeded by Sir Robert Carey, who served in the post until Queen Elizabeth's death in 1603. On the Scottish side of the line, in addition to the three March Wardens, there existed the important position of Keeper of Liddesdale, which from 1558 was held by James Hepburn, 4th Earl of Bothwell. He was succeeded by his nephew, Francis Stewart Bothwell, but when Francis fell from grace with James VI, his subsequent banishment in 1594 allowed Sir Walter Scott of Buccleuch to seize Bothwell's castle, Hermitage, and to succeed him as Keeper of Liddesdale. In this position, Buccleuch enjoyed equal status with the English Wardens of the Middle and West Marches, an arrangement that proved a source of great irritation to them. Lying between both West Marches was a narrow stretch of territory known as the Debateable Land. Although ownership of this piece of land had been argued over by both kingdoms for many years neither government was prepared to take responsibility for the inhabitants and consequently, it became a haven for miscreants who used it as a base for their depredations. Eventually, the area was more or less equally divided by an earthen rampart known as the Scot's Dyke, a bureaucratic solution that satisfied both governments, but did little to dampen the activities of the lawless residents.

The sums of money that Wardens were allowed by their respective governments had to pay for their accommodation, the upkeep of their servants, their food and drink and the salaries of their various officers. What was left over constituted the Warden's salary, which most of them found grossly inadequate. When Sir Ralph Eure requested a little financial assistance for the provision of 'a force of horsemen for defence' he was being optimistic, for Elizabeth I's treasurers were notoriously parsimonious and their delaying tactics were a constant source of frustration to Border officials. As a consequence, Wardens seem to have spent an inordinate amount of their time endeavouring to extract money from central government, not only for their own wages and those of their garrisons, but also for the maintenance of Border fortifications. In 1595, when Eure reported the arrest of 'one Robert

Ellot alias Hob of Bowholme, Scotsman', who was taken 'with the bloody hand by the Captain of Harbottle and has been arraigned and condemned to die for divers murders', he reminded the Lord Treasurer about the 'state and unfitness' of Hexham Gaol, part of which is 'newlie comde to the grounde... [so that] I am forced to pasture my owne house att dyvers tymes with suche [prisoners] as are of the better sorte!'

Wardens had various officers to assist them, including Deputies, Keepers, and Water Sergeants and Water Bailiffs, who were bound to keep 'the entrance of all men without licence out of either marche' and to 'carry messages or letters betwixt the Wardens'. The Warden also employed clerks to assist with his correspondence and to service the Warden's Courts. Setters and Searchers organized and monitored the 'Watches by the Fords' and Land Sergeants were tasked with apprehending those lawbreakers and fugitives to be presented at truce days.

Truce days were important events in the Warden's calendar, being the occasions when they met with their opposite numbers at locations close to the Borderline in order to discuss mutual business, address complaints and hopefully, present for trial individuals who had been accused of transgressions in the opposite realm. Under an assurance of safe conduct from sunrise of the day agreed upon to sunrise of the next, large numbers of spectators from both sides of the Border gathered to make merry and enjoy the inevitable rough justice that was meted out. As was to be expected, these meetings occasionally got out of hand and violence was quick to erupt, a good example being the skirmish in July 1575 between the followers of the English Warden Sir John Forster and his Scottish counterpart Sir John Carmichael that became known as the Raid of the Redeswire. 'From wordis they fell to strokis and manie war slain on both sides.'

'A Day of Truce'. Should an accused person not present themselves for trial at a truce day, men were often taken as 'pledges' to be held as hostages until the said person attended. On occasion, friends of the accused would offer themselves as 'pledges' and as a form of bail, headmen would pledge money for their friends or kinsmen. Artwork by Tom Scott RSA.

Looking back into the English Middle March near Hexpethgate, Windy Gyle, 'a meeting place of the Wardens of the Marches'. Other venues were usually 'for the East March the Hangingstone on Cheviot, or the Riding burn, the West ford at Norham, near Wark castle, at Carham or at Foulden-rig; for the Middle, Cocklaw, Stawford, the Reedswyre, Gamblespath at the head of Coquet; and for the Western, Keilder-stone, Rockcliffe and Kershopefoot.'

Due to the simmering hostility between the two nations, rumours of invasion and rebellion abounded. Spies were active in each realm and it was incumbent on the Warden to gather any intelligence that came his way and pass it on to his masters. One of the highlights in Sir John Forster's rather murky career was the apprehending of a man who claimed to be an itinerant dentist, but on closer questioning, turned out to possess information relating to 'the English enterprise', being the first indication of the forthcoming Spanish Armada.

On occasion, the Warden was also required to raise the country and ride with the 'Hot Trod', being the custom by which any Borderer who had been 'spoyled' could mount an immediate, if somewhat perilous, pursuit of his stolen goods into the opposite realm, the progress of which was signalled by a burning turf held aloft on a lance. Protocol relating to this 'fatal privilege' was meticulously laid down in the Border Laws and all men were legally obliged to follow the 'fray' and to be 'readie upon the first shout'. As we shall see, pursuit could sometimes turn into a hornets' nest and even when the Warden himself gave chase and was accompanied by the forces of law and order, Sir Robert Bowes warns that he could still be seriously outgunned by the opposition, for 'the country of North Tyndall, which is more plenished with wild and misdemeaned people, may make of men upon horseback and foot about six hundred, whereof there be commonly about two hundred able horsemen to ride with their keeper unto any service in Scotland'.

There was also the ever-present risk that whilst in the course of their duties, Border officers – and their troopers – would become the targets of deadly feud. Immediately following the execution of Geordie Burn, Sir Robert Carey incurred the enmity of 'the fyrebrande of the border', Sir Robert Kerr, Warden of the Scottish Middle March, under whose covert protection Burn had operated. Kerr was obviously not a man to cross as is evident from this 'conceipte' of him, written that same year by Sir Ralph Eure:

> Of his naturall disposition he is wyse, quicke spirited, perfect in Border causes, ambisious, desyorus to be greate... not able to maynteyne his estate to his greate mynd; attended by beggars and lowse persons, whose maynteynance is by thefte supported by his countenance, against whome if anie acte be done by anie Englysheman to the hurte or predudice of them, presentlie Sir Robert Kerr joyneth his force with his authorite to make revenge... what justice can the poor English subject expect?

Kerr's revenge followed swiftly by way of Scottish raids into the English East March and to make matters worse, Carey reports that shortly thereafter, Sir Cuthbert Collingwood,

> one of the chiefest gentlemen in Northumberland... upon a fray rose himself with his household servants and tennants and commyng where the theves were dryving his neighboures goodes, did his best to reskew them; and ere they parted one of the theves was slayne, which was a Burne, brother to this man I have now hanged. For whose death thus honestly done in defence of prince and country, he has had 17 of his tenants and servants slain, and himself driven to leave his home and live in the bishopric.

These miniatures of James Hepburn, 4th Earl of Bothwell 1535–78, and his wife, Lady Jean Gordon, Countess of Bothwell, 1544–1629, were commissioned in 1566 on the occasion of their wedding. Following their divorce a year later, Bothwell's ex-wife was eventually reunited with her first love, Alexander Ogilvie, and had a long and happy life. (Copyright Scottish National Portrait Gallery, Licensor www.scran.ac.uk)

Strangely enough, at a later date, whilst Sir Robert Kerr was serving as a 'pledge' or hostage, he chose to be lodged with Carey. In time, the two men became good friends and when Kerr was released, the pair 'met often at days of truce' and dispensed 'good justice'.

When the behaviour of the inhabitants of Liddesdale, Teviotdale, Tynedale, Redesdale and the like had been particularly outrageous, Wardens would mount official punitive raids, or 'Warden Roades' against them. In addition to punishing offenders, burning their homes and devastating the surrounding countryside, these large-scale raids were also an opportunity to supplement the Warden's income in the shape of prisoners taken for ransom, confiscated livestock, household gear and anything else that came to hand along the way. On occasion, these 'official' reprisal raids were carried out on a grand scale and executed with ruthless efficiency. In 1596, Lord Scrope, Warden of the English West March, was condemned by the Scottish Government for launching a brutal raid into Liddesdale.

> He sent and directed 2000 men, for the most part the Queen's waged men... who by his hounding out, invaded Liddesdale, raised fire and brent [burnt] 24 houses, and carried off all the goods within 4 miles of the bounds. They coupled the men their prisoners, tua and tua together, in a leashe like doggis. Of barnis and wemen three or fower scoore, they stripped of their clothis and sarkis [shirts], leaving them naked in that sort, exposit to the injurie of wind and weather, whereby nyne or tenne infants perished within eight daies thereafter.

More often than not, these inroads were carried out with the assistance of the riding surnames from the Warden's own March who, tempted by the prospect of 'legitimate' plunder, joined wholeheartedly in the enterprise. In October 1523, the Earl of Surrey wrote from Newcastle 'that Sir Rauf Fenwyke... and Sir William Heron', [Keepers of Redesdale and Tyndale] having enlisted the services of the Dodds, Milburns and Charltons, 'made two very good roodes [into Tevydale], and have gotten muche insight gear, catall, horse, and prisoners and returned without los'.

However, as Sir Ralph Fenwick was to find out, wheeling and dealing with powerful families such as the Charltons could prove a very 'ticklish' business and he soon found his former allies arrayed against him. Less than a year after his successful expedition into Teviotdale, Fenwick rode into Tynedale at the head of 80 horsemen with the intention of apprehending a lawbreaker named William Ridley. Quartering his troopers in Tarset Hall, his presence swiftly incurred the wrath of Ridley's friends. One of their headmen, William Charlton of Bellingham, 'having 200 of the seyde inhabitants of Tyndail reteigned, bound and bodily sworne upon a booke to him always to take hys parte, hering of the sayd Sir Rauff being ther, assembled parte of theim diligentely, and freshley set upon the said Sir Rauff, and not onely put him from hys purpose of attacking the sayd Ridley, but alsoe chased the sayd Sir Rauff out of Tyndaill, to his graet reproache'.

This affront to the king, in the person of 'Sir Rauff', could not go unpunished and was soon to be avenged by Thomas, Lord Dacre, acting Lord Warden of the Marches. Being a Border officer of some experience, Dacre was well aware that exercising a little give and take in his dealings with the riding surnames could prove extremely useful and at that point in time, he was suspected at Court of being overly indulgent towards certain Borderers. Seeing a chance to redeem himself, Dacre lost no time in seizing the said William Charlton along with his brother Roger Charlton and another of their kin named Thomas Charlton 'by whom all the inhabitants were governed, led, and ready at their commaundment'. Condemning these three 'hedesmen' as 'pledge-breakers' and receivers of stolen goods, Dacre ensured that William and Roger were judged and 'put to execution of dethe' without further delay. This swift and brutal approach certainly seems to have impressed the king who 'muche alloweth and commendeth [Dacre's] demeanor'. Having 'extinguished the rumour that he favoured evil doers' Dacre, no doubt relieved, found himself temporarily back in Royal favour.

Inevitably, some Border officials abused their privileges in furtherance of personal quarrels, none more so than Walter Scott of Buccleuch, the celebrated 'Bold Buccleuch', Keeper of Liddesdale and dangerous freebooter when it suited him. In 1595, Sir John Carey, Marshall of Berwick-upon-Tweed, wrote to Lord Burghley of Buccleuch's long-standing feud with the Charltons of Hesleyside.

> The quarrel Bucclughe hath to the Charletons is said to be this: Your honour knows... of a great rode that the Scottes... made upon Tyndale and Ridsdale, wherein they took up the whole country, and did very neare beggar them forever. Bucclughe and the rest of the Scottes having made some bragges and crackes, as the country durst scarse take anything of their own, but the Charletons being the sufficientest and ablest men uppon the Borders, did not only take theire own goodes agayne, but also so hartnd and perswaded theire neyghbors to take theirs, and not to be afraide, which hath ever synce stuck in Bucclughe's stomach, and this is the quarrel – for taking theire own!
>
> He makes another quarrel that long synce, in warr tyme, the Tyndale men... killed divers of his countrye, and... tooke awaye hys grandfathers shworde, and would never lett him have yt synce.

Numerous reports confirm that Buccleuch pursued this vendetta with great vindictiveness:

> Coming into the Myddle Marches to a place called Grenehugh, a wyddowes house in Tyndalle, where he sought for certen of the Charletons; and not fynding them he burned the house and all the corne in it and all that was therein, and so went hys way; he had in his company, as it is reported, very nere three hundred men, and within eight days afterward he came agayne to a place called the Bowte hill, and killed foure of the Charletons, very able and sufficient men and went his waye, threatening he would shortly have more of their lives.

Because the power and prestige attached to Border appointments was considerable, the positions attracted ambitious men and, on one occasion at least, allowed an unscrupulous rogue to manoeuvre himself – albeit briefly – into a role of national importance. As we have seen, along with the position of Keeper of Liddesdale went the grim fortress of Hermitage Castle and perhaps its most notorious resident was James Hepburn, 4th Earl of Bothwell, a man who was often in league with the wicked inhabitants of Liddesdale whose lawless behaviour he had been appointed to suppress. Following his

The brooding fortress of Hermitage guarded Liddesdale, the most lawless valley in the Scottish Border Marches. Here in their strong houses and towers dwelt the predatory Armstrongs, Elliots, Nixons and Crosiers, who were 'ever ryding' and 'very ill to tame'. Note the earthen gun platform in the foreground, which was erected in the 16th century.

near fatal encounter with Little Jock Elliot of the Park, Mary, Queen of Scots, 'despising all commodities of the way and weather and all danger of thieves' made her celebrated 50-mile (80km) ride from Jedburgh to Hermitage in order to visit the wounded Keeper, a journey that almost resulted in her death when, due to exposure, she contracted a serious illness. Although Bothwell was described as 'turbulent, licentious, brutal and unmannerly… the worst man at Court', Mary, Queen of Scots, obviously saw him in a somewhat kinder light and took him as her third husband, in spite of the fact that he was an undoubted accomplice in the murder of her second husband, Lord Darnley. As his ambition grew, many of the Scottish lairds turned against him and, ever the villain, Bothwell repaid the doomed queen's trust by deserting her after a humiliating confrontation with his enemies at Carberry Hill and fleeing into exile and imprisonment, never to return.

 THE EARL OF BOTHWELL AND LITTLE JOCK ELLIOT, 1566

On occasion, even unscrupulous officers like Bothwell had to present the face of law and order, and in 1566, at the head of 300 men, the Keeper of Liddesdale rounded up some of the worst 'limmers' (rascals) in his neighbourhood and promptly locked them up in Hermitage. Shortly afterwards, whilst out patrolling Bothwell 'chancit upon ane thief callit Johne Eluat [Little Jock Elliot] and schot him with ane dag'. However, when Bothwell approached the fallen reiver, he stumbled and Little Jock turned on him, inflicting upon the Keeper 'thrie woundis, ane in the bodie, ane in the heid, and ane in the hand'. Although badly wounded in the thigh, Jock appears to have made good his escape. When Bothwell was eventually found by his men and carried on a litter back to Hermitage, his misfortune deepened when the fortress was found to be under the control of the 'thievis and malefactouris of Liddesdale' who had been recently incarcerated there and had subsequently broken out and taken over the castle. Amidst acute embarrassment on Bothwell's part, a bargain was struck, the former prisoners were allowed to go free and the humiliated keeper was carried into his castle. Bothwell was destined to share in the downfall of Mary, Queen of Scots, and in 1578 his life ended in exile, imprisonment and madness. The Elliots, however, continued to thrive and the following year an obviously well recovered 'Scottis Joh of the Park' was being accused of sheep stealing at Jedburgh. Bothwell is attired as befits a gentleman of his status and is armed with a fine wheel lock pistol, the winding key for which is attached to his wrist. Jock grips a plain but obviously effective sword and for protection, wears a jack and a double-crested burgonet.

In this atmospheric painting by Tom Scott RSA, a party of raiders 'ride with the moonlight' and slip silently through the Border hills. This illustration accompanies *Whaup O' the Rede, a Ballad of the Border Raiders* by Will Ogilvie, published in 1909.

BELOW
Light to wear, highly protective and with an exceptionally good field of vision, the burgonet was perfectly suited to the reiver's activities on the Border Marches. This example, which has apparently been blackened against rusting, is of German origin and dates from around 1550. (IV. 475 Copyright The Board of Trustees of the Armouries)

BELOW RIGHT
Available in varying degrees of quality and often raised from a single piece of steel, the distinctive combed morion combined a robust construction with effective protection and was popular with foot-soldiers and cavalry alike. This helmet is of Italian manufacture and dates from the 1580s. (IV. 449 Copyright The Board of Trustees of the Armouries)

APPEARANCE AND EQUIPMENT

Judged by the military standards of the 16th century, the Borderer's equipment has been described as somewhat 'base and beggarly' and in a muster of the English Marches in 1584, a considerable number of horsemen are reported to be furnished with no more than 'jack, steil cap and spear'. Eleven years later, however, in the English Middle March, some 'soldiers' at least were furnished with 'coats of plaite, steele capps, skulls, lance staves, swordes and daggers and bows'. Shortly thereafter, the Bishop of Durham recommends to Lord Burghley that ideally, 'a horseman's furniture' should consist of 'a steele cap, a coate of plate, stockings and sleeves of plate, bootes and spurres; a Skottissh short sworde and a dagger, an horseman's staffe, and a case of pistolls'.

On the Scottish side of the Border, an Act of Parliament expected men to carry 'buklairs [small shields] and sweirds [swords], speirs of vi ells lang, [*c*.18ft – one Scottish ell = 37in.] Jedburghstavis [Jedburgh staves – polearms],

hagbuttis [harquebuses] and daggis [wheel lock pistols]'. However, many Borderers doubtless sallied forth on raids simply wearing their everyday clothing, perhaps with the protection of a stout leather doublet, and armed with no more than a lance, or 'staffe'. There is also evidence that many English Borderers carried the trusted longbow, whilst some Scots favoured the 'latch', a small crossbow popular with horsemen. For those that could afford it, the most popular item of protective clothing worn on the Border Marches was the 'jack of plaite'. The esteem in which this garment was held is confirmed by William Patten, an observer who accompanied the Duke of Somerset's great military expedition into Scotland in 1547. On the battlefield of Pinkie Cleugh, Patten reported that the Scots, including many of their nobility, were 'all clad a lyke in jackes', noting in addition that many carried 'swords... of exceeding good temper... made to slice'. Usually thigh length and sleeveless, the jack was constructed from two or three layers of quilted cloth between which were sewn small pieces of iron plate, the whole being faced with a robust material, such as fustian or leather. Being less cumbersome than plate armour and offering effective protection against cuts and slashes, the jack was ideally suited to the activities of a light horseman.

In spite of the increasing use of firearms in the late 16th century, mail still had its place on the battlefield. Whilst skirmishing against a force of English 'Bow-men and Arquebusiers' de Beaugue notes that when battle was joined, 'our Soldiers redoubled their Blows, and Sword in hand broke in upon the

Enemy with inexpressible Fury. They sustained little or no Loss by Fighting in this manner with the English, for they were all furnish'd with Headpieces and Coats of Mail, Arms most necessary to Arquebusiers by reason of the various Accidents which obliges them to come to handy-blows.'

ON CAMPAIGN

In 1596, it was observed that the English Middle March and most of the West were defended 'by high mountaynes and waste groundes all along the Border' thereby channelling any large-scale Scottish invasion through 'the East Marche... being smaller and weaker than either of the others... thorowe a plaine... countrey very nere adjoyninge, and sometimes by the river of Twede, which is full of foordes'. However, the remote 'mountaynes' and 'wastes' were perfect cover for the small raiding parties that slipped under cover of darkness through the maze of Border hills and river valleys. It seems that these men, who were Border-bred and had intimate knowledge of the terrain, favoured certain 'secret passages' and in 1597, a *Breafe of the Ways and Passages of the Middle Marche* includes mention of 'a place called the Gribbheade, a passage and hye way for the theefe; joining on the west ende of Chiveat and one mile distant from Hexpethe, another passage at Hexpeth gate heade called the Coklaw... where days of Marche be holden and another passage at the Readeswire.' The *Breafe* also includes over 20 'passages of the Scottes all along Rydsdayle', including the colourfully named 'Hell cauldron-borne-foote, from Bell kirk', 'Hangingstone from Buttrod head' and a passage from Tynedale known as 'Murders rack from Blackup saughs'. Kershope Bridge seems to have been much used by raiders of both kingdoms and, in 1550, was described as 'a common waye as well for the theves of Tyndall, Bewcastle, and Gilsland in England, as for theves of Liddesdale in Scotland [who] with there stollen goodes [pass] from th' one realm to th' other'. On occasion, ambitious raiders probed deep into the opposite realm, where peaceable citizens were ill prepared to deal with them. In 1595, it was reported that a raiding party of 'Ellottes' from Liddesdale, riding 'along the hyer partes of the rivers of Tease, Weare and Darwent', had taken a prisoner out of his house near Durham

D **THE BORDER REIVER, 16TH CENTURY**
1. burgonet
2. combed morion
3. cabasset
4. steel cap or 'skull'
5. basket-hilted sword, 1540; rapier, late 16th century; broadsword, late 15th century
6. sword and hanger
7. ballock daggers and parrying dagger
8. small crossbow or 'latch'
9. lance or 'staff'
10. wheel lock pistol or 'dagg'
11. 'jack of plaite' and method of construction
12. war saddle with two holstered 'daggs'
13. fully equipped reiver, ready for a foray.

and were currently holding him for ransom in Liddesdale. 'Sundry attempts' were also made on 'two wealthy men's houses near Richmond, 70 miles from the Border', and one of them 'spoyled', much to the 'disquiet and terror' of the local population!

It was from the beginning of October until the middle of March that Lord Wharton, Lord Deputy General of the English Middle Marches, ordered 'watch to be kept throughout the whole extent of the Border, by day on the heights, by night at the fords'. Writing in 1597, Sir Robert Carey called this period 'the theves harvest' and notes that:

This well-used basket-hilted broadsword provides good protection for the hand and is representative of the quality of weapon that must have been carried by many on the Border Marches. Note the way the sword is slung and the wearer's robust, homespun clothing. (The Borderers)

This swept-hilt rapier has a wired grip and a knuckle guard of twisted steel bars. Such weapons, which were often used in conjunction with a parrying dagger, saw increasing use in the latter part of the 16th century.

> They will never lightly steale hard before Lammas [1 August] for fear of the assizes, but being once past, they returne to their former trade, and, unles in such years as they cannot ride upon the wastes by reason of stormes and snowes, the last moneths of the yeare are theyr chieffe time of steallinge, for then are the nightes longest, theyr horses hard at meat and will ride best, cattell strong and will drive furthest. After Candlemass [2 February] the nightes grow shorte, and cattell grow weake, and oates growing dearer, they feed theyr horses worse, and quickly turn them out to grasse.

In 1327, the chronicler Jean Froissart left us with this description of a Scottish army that invaded the North of England and his comments regarding the habits of the 'common people' and how they conducted themselves whilst on campaign are of particular interest.

> These Scottish men are... armed after their guise, right hardy and fierce, for they are all a-horseback... the common people... on little hackneys and geldings... which were never tied nor kept at hard meat, but let go to pasture in the fields and bushes. They take with them no purveyance of bread nor wine, for their usage and soberness is such in time of war, that they will pass in the journey a great long time with flesh half sodden, without bread, and drink of the river water without wine, and they neither care for pots nor pans, for they seethe [cook] beasts in their own skins... on their horse between the saddle and the panel they truss a broad plate of metal, and behind the saddle they will have a little sack full of oatmeal, to the intent that when they have eaten of the sodden flesh that their stomachs seem weak and feeble, then they lay this plate on the fire and temper a little of the oatmeal; and when the plate is hot, they cast of the thin paste thereon, and so make a little cake in manner of a cracknell or biscuit, and that they eat to comfort withal their stomachs. Wherefore it is no great marvel [that] they make greater journeys than other people do.

In all probability, later generations of raiders, both Scottish and English, transported and sustained themselves in a very similar manner.

Without doubt, the most colourful and descriptive account of the reiver going about his business comes from Bishop Leslie, who tells us:

They sally out of their own borders, in the night, in troops through unfrequented by-ways, and many intricate windings. All the day time, they refresh themselves and their horses in lurking holes they have pitched upon before, till they arrive in the dark at those places they have a design upon. As soon as they have seized upon the booty, they, in like manner, return home in the night, through blind ways, and fetching many a compass. The more skilful any captain is to pass through those wild deserts, crooked turnings, and deep precipices, in the thickest mists and darkness, his reputation is the greater, and he is looked upon as a man of an excellent head.

Should things go badly wrong, it seems the reivers still had one or two cards left to play. The bishop continues:

And they are so very cunning, that they seldom have their booty taken from them... unless sometimes, when, by the help of blood-hounds following them exactly upon the tract, they may chance to fall into the hands of their adversaries. When being taken, they have so much persuasive eloquence, and so many smooth and insinuating words at their command, that if they do not move their judges, nay, and even their adversaries (notwithstanding the severity of their natures), to have mercy, yet they incline them to admiration and compassion.

Perhaps the commonest weapon carried on the Border Marches was the ballock dagger. This man carries a fine example that comes replete with two smaller knives; the decorative silver panels on the belt and sheath are based on archaeological finds around Old Buittle Tower.

Such men drove officials to despair. Writing in the 1580s, Sir John Selby reports 'These Liddesdale men are the most disordered of all the Border, they come in great bands through Tevedall and the Marc [Merse] into these East Marches and return with their booty quietly the same way, without resistance, for they have no Warden to answer for them by Border Law.' In 1595, Lord Scrope wrote of the West March, 'this wardenry is too weak for offence or defence, especially Bewcastle, through long continued incursions without redress. Thus Liddesdale passes easily through it to attack Gilsland, which place is also greatly weakened from the same cause.'

It is apparent that a large number of these forays appear to have gone unchallenged by a system of law enforcement that seems to have been overwhelmed by the sheer volume of criminality, which reached its zenith in the latter part of the 16th century. In 1597, the Bishop of Durham, whilst questioning the competence of Sir Ralph Eure, Warden of the English Middle March, and Mr Percy, Constable of Alnwick and Morpeth castles, was moved to ask 'how it comes that... Scottish and English thieves are quietly allowed to ride from the head of Liddisdale through Redesdale, to the very sea syde at and about Warkwork [Warkworth], as it were traverse by a diameter throughout Northumberland over and over, againe and againe, without impeachment?' In understandable exasperation, he concludes 'I wish myself once quit of these troublesome border affairs!'

Brawling was fairly commonplace in Border towns and these two men are well prepared for just such an eventuality. The man on the right attacks with a sword and parrying dagger, whilst his opponent defends himself with a combination of sword and buckler.

However, most Wardens and their officers endeavoured to conduct themselves in a diligent manner and took what measures they could to staunch the flow of raiding. Writing to Lord Burghley in 1595, Sir Ralph Eure, acting on the advice of 'experienced men here', advocated 'a general watch of the fords and passages of this whole [Middle] March, which is now begun, and will be continued so long as we find it dothe any good'. However, eliciting help from some quarters proved quite difficult and, in February 1595, Eure wrote to Lord Burghley urging him to 'command the gentlemen of great living and fair houses on the March, to.... maintain a sufficient number of horse and men furnished to rise to the frays for defence', adding reproachfully, 'this would both strengthen the country and remove them from their quiet dwellings in the Bishopric and Yorkshire whither they have had to repair from their "unmeasureable losse". I have arranged with them that watchmen attend the beacons to fire them in case of sudden incursions.' The following year, the ever-beleaguered Eure, who was clearly unsuited to the rigours of his post, was writing to Burghley again, lamenting the 'rewdnes' of the country and complaining that he still 'cannot get the [local] gentlemen to keep watch or skowre the waistes with their tenants and neighbours', adding

E **BORDER HORSE IN IRELAND, 1595**

In a series of campaigns that followed the Earl of Tyrone's rebellion against English rule in Ireland, Border horsemen were sometimes led by their own 'headmen' who held the rank of captain. Skirmishing against warriors as wily and ruthless as themselves, both sides showed little mercy to their opponents. These two Borderers, both well wrapped against the weather, admire the great sword carried by a slain 'galloglas', a mercenary soldier from the Scottish West Highlands, whose costume and weapons are taken from an illustration by Albrecht Durer dated 1521. The appearance of the trooper (left) is based on an illustration from John Derricke's *Image of Ireland*, published in 1581. He is armed with a lance and wears a coat of mail, long leather riding boots and a burgonet. His oval shield, bearing the cross of St George, is slung from his saddle. His 'headman', who carries a wheel lock pistol, also wears stout leather riding boots and protects himself with a fine morion-burgonet and a 'back and breast', which is visible beneath his heavy 'cassock' coat.

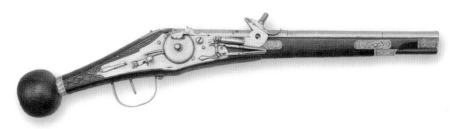

This man is equipped with a caliver, powder and shot. Such firearms saw increasing use near the end of the 16th century. In 1596, Sir Ralph Eure desired that 'a proportion of shotte might be allotted, as in Haltewisell 20, Haydon bridge 12, Hexham 30, Bellingham 8 or 10, Morpeth 50 or 60, Alnwick 80 or 100. Others in the country might be bowmen, others with halberds, lances or pikes.' (The Borderers)

indignantly that these same gentlemen were greatly discontented by his orders regarding the handing over of prisoners taken within the March to the Warden's officers. With an eye firmly on ransom, these 'gentlemen' pointed out in no uncertain terms that 'they do not hazard their lives to benefit others not at the capture!'

As Eure was aware, the 'assistance' given by local riding families could prove to be a double-edged sword, but the help of trustworthy local men could prove invaluable. In 1597, when he was under suspicion of misappropriating funds destined for the hiring of troopers from Yorkshire, Eure explains himself as follows.

As the Yorkshire men were removed by want of... death or offences, I replaced them by countrymen or my servants... as they knew the wastes for my secret guidance when needed... the native countrymen are better at handling spears etc. on horseback than the Yorkshire or bishopric men, better prickers in a chase as knowing the mosses, more nimble on foot and some keep 'slewe dogges' to serve the country, which the country could not have paid for. Also, divers of them lie in the 'highe streate', where the malefactors pass, not 4 or 5 miles out of Hexham next the waste, and few are landed or rich men, and failing the pay, cannot keep horses. These men in pay [are] always ready to the fray.

The use of 'slewe dogges', or bloodhounds, to track down raiders and stolen livestock is often mentioned and it was decreed that these dogs were 'to be kept in convenient places and money levied, or an allowance, to maintain them'. Such beasts were obviously regarded as prized possessions and looked after accordingly.

Bridges were chained to deter raiders, fords were guarded and a system of beacons was maintained on both sides of the Border. On the approach of marauders, beacons, which were situated on hillsides and on the 'tops' of tower houses, were lit to spread a warning across the Border Marches. On occasion, these measures worked to deadly effect. In January 1528, William Charleton of Shitlyngton Hall and Archibald Dodd, with two Scotsmen, Harry Noble and Roger Armestrong, set out on a foray into the Bishopric of Durham. Picking up five companions along the way they came to the neighbourhood of Woolsingham, where they abducted the parson of Muggleswick and carried him off for ransom. As the raiders made their way homeward, they were unable to resist plundering three dwellings at

Penwoodside whereby the alarm was raised and the local population, led by the Bailiff of Hexham, rose against them. The Earl of Northumberland relates their subsequent fate to Cardinal Wolsey:

> The water of Tyne was that night one great flode, so that the sayd theves couth not passe the same at no fordes, but were driven of necessitie to a brygge within a lordship of myne called Aydon Brygge, which by my commaundment was barred, chained, and lokked faste, so that the sayd theves couth not passe with their horses over the same, but were constrained to leave their horses behynde them, and flee away on foote. And upon the same a servaunte of myne, called Thomas Errington, ruler of my tenants in those quarters, persewed after theyme with a sleueth hounde, to the which pursuitte of theyme, after the crye in aid, came to theyme… diverse other inhabitants of Tyndaill to helpe to put down those rebellious persons, which forwardness in oppressing mallifactors hath not been sene aforetyme in Tyndaill men.

In the ensuing pursuit William Charleton and Harry Noble were hunted down and slain by Thomas Errington, whilst Roger Armestrong and Archie Dodd were taken and executed. The other five members of the gang somehow seem to have evaded capture. Charleton's corpse was hung in chains at Hexham, Noble's on Haydon Bridge and the bodies of Armestrong and Dodd shared similar fates at Newcastle and Alnwick.

When raiders were returning homeward following a profitable night's work, the stolen cattle and sheep they were driving before them would have considerably hampered their progress. It was at these times, whilst playing cat and mouse with the local watches and the Warden's roving patrols, that their familiarity with the surrounding terrain could tip the balance in their favour. However, given the amount of criminal activity on the Border Marches, reiving bands undoubtedly passed each other in the night and, occasionally, one band fell victim to another, as reported by George Heron of Chipchase in 1565.

The wicked-looking polearm carried by this 'foot loon' was known as a 'Jeddart staff'. In 1596, Lord Scrope reported that Buccleuch had armed his followers with 'more muskettes, calivours, horsemens staves, and shorte Jedburgh staves for footemen, than betokens quietness… I suspect the worst'. Note the shield, or vamplate, attached to the shaft, which gave protection to the hands.

> Lyiddesdaill is myndyt to mayk misorder and to do the evel that they can in these quarters. I knowe theye cannot doe it without the helpe of some, both of Tyndaill and Rydesdaill, as they have had even now this last Fryday night, when they dyd take up Swethope. For one parte of them went away thorow Tendall with the prisoners, and another thorow Ryddesdail with the nowt [cattle]. And the theves off Tyndaill that wis goyng estelling [a stealing] into Scotland, found the Scotts with the nowt lying in shells [shielings] at Uttenshope, in Ryddisdaill. And when the theves off Tyndaill perceived the Scotts were at rest, they stale the nowt, from the Scotts, and in the morning when the Scotts mest the nowt they dyd com into Reddisdayll again, to boro a dog to follo, and theye got knowledge whyche of Tyndaill had the nowt.

Sometimes, local forces bold enough to mount a pursuit found they were ill equipped and too small in numbers to actually confront the reiving bands they were pursuing. This apparent shortage of ably furnished men was of great concern to Sir Ralph Eure. Whilst pleading for extra cash with which to 'furnish' Northumbrian tenants in a fitting manner, he writes 'I myself viewed the footmen in the most part of the country – which veiwe dothe greatly discomforte me. What they have at home I know not, but at muster some bring a steel cap and light horseman's staff, most without cap, or ought els but a staff – and so the country is furnished.' In March 1595, Eure reports a foray 'by some Scots of Jedworth forest… who took 20 head of cattle from Widow Milburne of the Heighfield in Tyndale, and the poor widow prisoner, with her children and servants. The fray rose, and the country followed, but for want of horse to go nearer, they stood on a hill and saw the Scots dividing

This well-mounted Border laird is armed with a lance, ballock dagger and holstered 'dagg'. He wears a 'steill bonnett' over an arming cap, a fine doublet, slashed hose and gloves. Note the small leather boot attached to his stirrup in which the butt of his lance rests and the strap attached to the lance shaft, which can be looped around the arm, thus enabling the use of both hands whilst riding.

their goods, but were not strong enough to set on them.' Undeterred, the intrepid Tynedalers 'passed another way to [Jedworth] forest and on their return, being not above 8 horse, the rest foot, they brought away 60 head of beastes, although the Scots, horse and foot, rose and fronted them for 3 or 4 miles, but fought not.'

There was, however, always the danger that resistance, no matter how justified, could provoke acts of increasingly violent retaliation. In April 1597, Sir Robert Carey reports to the Privy Council:

On the 14th instant at night, 4 Scotsmen broke up a poor man's doors at Killam on this March, taking his cattle; the town followed, rescued the goods, sore hurt 3 of the Scots, and brought them back prisoners. The 4th Scot raised his country meanwhile, and at daybreak 40 horse and foot attacked Killam, but being resisted by the town, who behaved themselves very honestly, they were driven off and two more taken prisoners. Whereon the Scots raised Tyvidale, being near hand, and to the number of 160 horse and foot came back by 7 in the morning, and not only rescued all the prisoners, but slew a man, left seven for dead, and hurt very sore a great many others.

When raiders sallied forth in large numbers, many Border folk were left with no choice but to leave their homes and seek refuge in the surrounding hills, mosses, woods and moorlands with whatever goods and chattels they could carry. To these great confederations of reivers, affluent towns were tempting targets. The people of Peebles, having seen their town burnt by English forces in 1549, built a surrounding wall for protection, but in 1583 the Armstrongs, Grahams, Elliots and Johnstones still managed to inflict

In the early 17th century, in spite of the increasing use of firearms, the tried and trusted longbow remained in service throughout the Borders. Raiders would have been skilled archers and from the saddle, could rapidly inflict devastating injuries with a variety of arrows.

'greit injuris on the townsfolk of Peebles'. It was, therefore, against all comers that between the hours of 9pm and 4am 'the half quarter of the toon' had 'to watch nightly while the moon grows to proud light, and… watch each night as long as the moon is proud'. This obligation fell on 'the principal of each house or else a sufficient man in his place' and in the event of 'any sudden fray to the town, by incursions of thieves or enemies… all neighbours to convene well armed'.

When the worst came to the worst, some towns could mount a spirited defence, as did the folk of Haltwhistle in Northumberland when they were attacked by a war band of Armstrongs from Liddesdale. (The incident was subsequently celebrated in the ballad 'The Fray of Hautwessel'.) Sir Robert Carey tells us:

Thither they came, and set many houses of the town on fire, and took away all their goods; and as they were running up and down the streets with lights in their hands to set more houses on fire, there was one other of the Ridleys that was in a strong stone house that made a shot out amongst them, and it was his good hap to kill an Armstrong, one of the sons of the chiefest outlaw. The death of this young man [Wat Armstrong] wrought so deep an impression amongst them, as many vows were made that before the end of next winter they would lay the whole border waste… the chief of all these outlaws was old Sim of Whittram. He had five or six sons as able men as the borders had. This old man and his sons had not so few as two hundred at their commands that were ever ready to ride with them to all actions at their beck.

Shortly thereafter, in his capacity as Warden of the English Middle March, Carey made a retaliatory raid into Liddesdale and carried off goods belonging to the Armstrongs which were then distributed amongst those folk in Haltwhistle who had been 'spoyled' by the raiders. Of all the Wardens in post at the tail end of the 16th century, Carey seems to have been best suited to the job. He had seen active service in France at the capture of Arques and following a rather dull period at Elizabeth's court, secured an appointment as Deputy Warden of the West March. Writing in his memoirs, his enthusiasm for his new life is clearly evident: 'I took myself to the country where I lived with great comfort: for we had a stirring world, and few days passed over my head but I was on horseback, either to prevent mischief, or to take malefactors.'

Following his successful expedition against the Armstrongs, Carey decided to press home his advantage and take the fight into the reivers' own backyard. In July 1601, with the blessing of James VI of Scotland, he set out 'to apprehend some of these Liddesdale outlaws… amongst the bogs, moors and woods hitherto thought impregnable'. From his memoirs, he writes:

Horse furniture would have consisted of a deep war saddle that enabled a rider to keep his seat whilst engaged in combat, along with a girth, irons, numnah, crop, bridle, bardings and a saddlecloth. Riders would also carry a canvas water bucket, a tether, rope halter, picket spike, hay net and a bag for oats. Note the pair of holstered 'daggs' and powder flask.

My intention… was that myself with my two deputies, and the forty horse that I was allowed, would with what speed we could make ourselves ready to go up to the wastes, and there we would entrench ourselves, and lie as near as we could to the outlaws… and I did not doubt before the summer ended, to do something that should abate the pride of these outlaws.

Those that were unwilling to hazard themselves liked not this motion… but there were divers young gentlemen that offered to go with me, some with three, some with four horses, and to stay with me so long as I would there continue. I… found that with myself, my officers, the gentlemen and our servants, we should be about two hundred good men and horse; a competent number as I thought for such a service. The day and place was appointed for our meeting in the wastes and by the help of the foot of Liddesdale and Ridsdale, we had soon built a pretty fort, and within it we had all cabins to lie in, and every one brought beds or mattresses to lie on. There we stayed from the middle of June till almost the end of August… we wanted no provision for ourselves nor our horses; for the country people were well paid for anything they brought us, so that we had a good market every day before our fort, to buy what we lacked.

The chief outlaws at our coming fled their houses, where they dwelt, and betook themselves (with all their goods), to a large and great forest which was called the Tarras. It was of that strength, and so surrounded by bogs and marshy grounds, and thick bushes and shrubs, as they feared not the force, nor power of England, nor Scotland, so long as they were there. The time I stayed at the fort I was not idle, but cast by all means I could how to take them in the great strength they were in. I found a means to send a hundred and fifty horsemen into Scotland (conveyed by a muffled man not known to any of the company) thirty miles within Scotland, and the business was so carried that none in the country took any alarm at this passage. They were quietly brought to the back [Scottish] side of the Tarras… and there they divided themselves into three parts, and took up three passages which the outlaws made themselves secure of if from the England side they should at any time be put at.

Across the region, the reiver's horse was variously known as a 'galloway', 'hobbler' and 'bog-trotter'. Sure footed and with great stamina, these sturdy ponies were capable of carrying the reiver great distances across Border mosses, bogs and moorland and were highly regarded by outlaws and lawmen alike.

They had their scouts on the tops of hills on the English side to give them warning if at any time any power of men should come to surprise them. The three ambushes were… laid without being discovered and about four o'clock in the morning there were three hundred horse and a thousand foot that came directly to the place where the scouts lay. They gave the alarum: our men brake down as fast as they could into the wood. The outlaws thought themselves safe, assuring themselves at any time to escape; but they were so strongly set upon on the English side as they were forced to leave their goods and to betake themselves to their passages towards Scotland. There were presently five taken of the principal of them. The rest, seeing themselves (as they thought) betrayed, retired into the thick woods and bogs, that our men durst not follow them, for fear of losing themselves. The principal of the five that were taken were two of the eldest sons of Sim of Whitram. These five they brought to me to the fort, and a number of goods both of sheep and kine [cattle], which satisfied most part of the country that they had stolen them from. The five that were taken were of great worth and value amongst them, insomuch that for their liberty I should have what conditions I should demand or desire... and so upon these conditions I set them at liberty, and was never after troubled with these kind of people. Thus... we brake up our fort, and every man retired to his own home.

BELIEF AND BELONGING

The majority of respectable Borderers – and thieves – were farmers. Their livelihood depended on the rearing and breeding of cattle, sheep and horses, although hogs and goats were also kept. The custom of 'summering', or transhumance, was practised, which involved the seasonal movement of their animals to higher pastureland. 'Here every year', wrote the Elizabethan antiquarian William Camden, 'round about in the wastes as they terme them... you may see, as it were, the ancient Nomads, a martiall kind of men, who frome the moneth of Aprill unto August, lye out scattering and summering (as they tearme it), with their cattle in little cottages here and there which they call Sheals, or Shealings.' However, although this period was of 'chefest profitt' to the Borderer, the constant threat of marauders could occasionally force him to abandon his 'sommer sheale'.

Surprisingly enough, many Scots found legitimate work in the English Marches, some being employed as shepherds or fishermen whilst others made their living in the towns of Berwick and Carlisle manufacturing saddles, bridles, stirrups and skins for the covering of plate armour. Although they seem to have been tolerated by the local population, it would appear they were much suspected of being spies. In towns, poverty led to petty theft, or 'pyking', and in the mid-16th century we hear of one Cristian Fairle of Peebles, who was suspected of 'pyking' hens and also for taking a shirt from James Stewart which he (subsequently) took off her back when she was wearing it! Apparently, some Borderers dwelling near the coast were not averse to a little piracy and even members of the Berwick garrison were accused of aiding and abetting pirates. 'Coyning' was another way of topping up finances and men from the Berwick garrison (again) seemed to have developed a talent for counterfeiting Scots money, a practice that was seemingly 'wynked at' by their Warden, Lord Hunsdon.

The Borderer's personal wealth was certainly reflected in his clothing and those with the means attired themselves accordingly. William Anesley of East Shaftoe, a Northumberland gentleman, owned 'twoo jackets, twoo dubletts, twoo paire of hose, foore shirtes, one hatt and one blake Spanish cappe'. Others further down the social ladder made do with 'lether jerkyns', 'canevas

This well-attired gentleman from Tynedale could be a merchant of some standing or perhaps even a Knight of the Shire. He wears a Tudor cap and beneath an expensive loose over-gown, is dressed in an embroidered leather doublet, a linen shirt and ruff, wool hose and baggy 'Venetian' breeches. He wears robust leather shoes, or 'latchets', and for defence against footpads, chooses to carry a blackthorn cudgel.

This gentleman is fashionably dressed in a tall felt hat with buckled hatband and, over a linen shirt with ruffed collar and cuffs, wears a wool doublet that is laced at the waist to black panelled trunk hose. His leather sleeveless jerkin is 'pinked' (punch decoration) and his legs are protected by bucket-top leather riding boots. Suspended from his sword belt is a swept-hilt rapier.

doblets', 'grograyne briches', 'knyte hoes', a 'payre of bootes' and if they were lucky, 'a best Jackett'.

Not surprisingly, the Borderer's home reflected his turbulent way of life and was built with security firmly in mind. The popular option for the Border laird was the tower house, which usually comprised four or five storeys of accommodation carried over an immensely strong barrel-vaulted basement that was used for storage. Standing about 40–60ft (12.2–18.3m) high with stone walls averaging around 5–10ft (1.5–3m) thick and measuring around 30 by 40 ft (9.1 by 12.2m), the building was topped with a stone flagged roof and a battlemented parapet. Entry was generally at ground level via a small, stout wooden door and an inner gate of iron latticework known as a 'yett'. A spiral staircase in a corner of the building allowed access to the upper floors, and windows were invariably small, barred and well above ground level. Tower houses were usually enclosed by a stone wall known as a 'barmkin' and within this perimeter were ancillary buildings, such as a hall and a kitchen.

The wealthier farmer and his family could choose to live with some degree of security in a defensible farmhouse known as a bastle. These two-storey rectangular buildings had stone walls averaging 3–4ft (1–1.2m) thick and were around 30–33ft (9–10m) by 16–18ft (5.5–6m). The upper floor, which provided the family's accommodation, was carried over a barrel-vaulted basement or was supported on substantial oak beams. Most bastles were roofed with stone slabs and had two or three small windows set high up in their walls. The ground floor, which was used to secure valuable animals in times of trouble, was entered through a small door in the gable end of the building and, once the door was bolted shut from the inside, access to the upper floor was by ladder, through a small trapdoor in the ceiling, which could then be locked down. External access to the upper floor was via a strong wooden door, situated well above ground level, which was reached by climbing a ladder that could be retracted by the last man through.

Another option available to the minor Border headman was the 'pele'. The walls of these incredibly robust buildings were constructed with massive oak tree trunks and were topped off with a roof of thick turves, the dwelling being enclosed by a stout palisade. Sir Robert Bowes, in his survey of the Borderland in 1542, informs us that for security, 'a great number of these… houses [are] set so together in one quarter, that a fray or outcry made in one house may warn all the residue'. None of these buildings could withstand a serious assault or prolonged siege, but they could prove an effective deterrent against small raiding parties that would hopefully move on in search of easier

pickings. Poorer folk would appear to have lived in fairly squalid conditions, and in 1569 a house in Liddesdale belonging to John Armstrong of the Side was haughtily described as a 'cottage not to be compared to many a dog kennel in England'.

According to Bishop Leslie, the Scots lived mainly on 'flesh, milk, cheese and parched barley... having little use of bread, good beer or wine'. Some tower houses, however, incorporated within their barmkin a 'brew house', and in the homes of such men as William Kerr of Ancrum might be found 'clarret' and 'quhyte wyne'. Because water was not always safe to drink, beer was often drunk in its place. In spite of Bishop Leslie's observation to the contrary, both sexes seem to have enjoyed the drink and in 1595 James VI of Scotland took delivery of '12 tuns of double London beer, for his dearest spouse [who] is daily accustomed to drink of the same'. The lady had obviously developed quite a taste for that particular brew and in 1596 the king was ordering another 30 tuns. Over indulgence seems to have been a problem for some and in 1595, Sir Robert Carey has this to say of Sir John Forster's 'basterd sun... wan that is so given over to drunkennes, that if he cannot get company, he will sit in a chayre in his chamber and drinke him self drunke before he reise!'

In their leisure time, the upper classes enjoyed hunting and hawking and a Border laird would be entertained by 'pipars', or 'tail tellaris' and might indulge in an occasional game of 'kyles' (skittles), or chance his luck 'at the cartis'. Horse races and football matches were frequently held in the Border Marches and proved popular with rogues and worthies alike. Drawing large crowds, these sporting events were prone to ending in heavy drinking and violence and in 1602 one quarrel at least was resolved with 'pistols and hackbuts'. In spite of their turbulent lifestyle, the Borderers had a strong tradition of storytelling, music and poetry. The Border ballads, which give us a vivid insight into life on the Border Marches, were collected and preserved by Sir Walter Scott in the mid-19th century and recount in colourful prose the

ABOVE LEFT
At the bottom of the social ladder were the 'lawless persons' mentioned in so many complaints and reports. This man wears a wool split-brim statute cap, a coarse linen shirt and is protected by a padded arming jack and a locally wrought 'back and breast'. His weapon, however, is a keen-edged broadsword of quality.

ABOVE
In 1585, a prosperous merchant's wife in Newcastle owned 'a gowne, one kyrtle, a petycote, one payre of newe sleves... a read hatt and a cape'. Although this woman's garments are rather more serviceable, they were apparently comfortable enough to wear. She wears a wool high collared 'partlet', a linen gown which is pointed to a boned bodice, a green linen apron fastened with a tie, and beneath her outer garments, wool hose and a linen shift. In the interest of hygiene linen undergarments would be washed regularly. Note her belt, eating knife and needle case.

Football, which was a dangerous, rough and tumble version of today's sport, was certainly popular in the Border Marches and matches seem to have taken place on the common greens near towns and villages. There appear to have been few rules, no recognized boundaries and the number of players seems to have varied from a mob of between 200 or 300, to six Armstrongs who came to play a match against six Englishmen at Bewcastle. (Illustration by Angus McBride, courtesy of The Historic Hexham Trust)

exploits of the reiving brotherhood. Rich in high drama, often with tragic overtones, these ballads would have been recited by travelling storytellers at social gatherings such as truce days, fairs, weddings and funerals.

Religion, or perhaps the lack of it, also played its part in Border life. Tradition has it that a traveller, noting the absence of a single chapel in Liddesdale, is reported to have asked the question 'Are there any Christians here?' The scathing reply rang out 'Na, we're a' Elliots and Armstrangs!' However, Bishop Leslie does tell us that such men did pray devoutly enough before setting out on a raid!

Writing from Newcastle in 1595, Sir William Bowes, a Border commissioner, notes 'That true religion hath verie little place, not by the unwillingness of the people to heare, but by the want of meanes, scant three able preachers being found in the whole country'. As a consequence, Border communities were often served by priests of questionable character and in 1561, it was reported that amongst the 'superstitious people on the Borders, priests go with sword, dagger and such coarse apparel as they can get, not being

 THE GREAT HALL, 1590s

In 1598, an English traveller who was the guest of a Scottish Border laird, having declared that he was cared for 'after their best manner' left the following observations. 'Many servants brought in the meat, with blue caps on their heads, the table being more than half furnished with great platters of porridge, each having a little sodden meat… the upper mess instead of porridge had a pullet with some prunes in the broth.' He further notes that 'the Scots, living then in factions, used to keep many followers and so consumed their revenues in victuals and were always in want of money'. There could be an interesting mix of company in such Border holds and in the 1570s two English spies, Francis Haugh and Robert Constable, spent some time at Ferniehirst Castle socializing with the Kerrs, drinking ale and 'playing at the cards' with 'many guests of divers factions, some outlaws of England, some of Scotland, some neighbours thereabout'. In this scene set in the great hall of a Scottish tower house, a disagreement has broken out between one of the players and the well-attired laird – a Scott from the heraldic device above the hearth – much to the amusement of the 'counterfeit priest' and his 'concubine'. Note the flustered ladies in the window seat, the servants in the background and the 'pyper' who sits beside the hearth.

curious what colour or fashion it be'. In 1498, the Bishop of Durham writes 'Nay, the priests of that country [Tynedale and Redesdale] are most evil, they keep their concubines, they are irregular, suspended, excommunicated, and interdicted clergy… and some are not ordained at all, but merely counterfeits of priests, and they dare to celebrate the Holy Sacrifice in profane and ruined places, with vestments torn, ragged, and most filthy.' In 1536, at Brinkburn Priory, Northumberland, Henry VIII's commissioners found that one William Hogeson, the Prior, was 'incontinent with divers women' and under the Act of Dissolution, the house was dissolved and the dissolute Prior pensioned off with £11 per year. However, when an exasperated clergy eventually withdrew its blessing and interdicted the 'chyrches of Tindaill' Hector Charlton, 'one of their capeteynes', took matters into his own hands and 'resaved the parsonnes dewties and served them all of wyne… and got a Scotch friar to give the Sacrament to a number of evil disposed people'.

As an antidote to these less than perfect men of the cloth, we hear of the dedicated Master Bernard Gilpin, who became known as 'The Apostle of the North'. Each year, near Christmas time, Gilpin ventured forth from his parish at Houghton-le Spring in Durham to spread God's Word to the people of the Borders. In the face of much adversity, he remained steadfast in his mission to bring spiritual enlightenment to the 'perverse' and 'crooked' population, settling some of their feuds and even building a school and 'allowing maintenance for master and usher and privately instructing some of the best scholars himself'. Sadly, in spite of Gilpin's heroic endeavours, it was apparent to all concerned that 'his work was but a tiny drop of oil poured on an ocean of ignorance'.

The Bishop of Glasgow laid a long and extraordinary curse on the reivers and excommunication seems to have been threatened and invoked on many an occasion. We find that various Milburns, Robsons and Dodds were to be released from sentences of excommunication on condition 'of their abstaining from theft in the future' and because such men were invariably armed when they attended a service, 'nor shall they enter a church, or place consecrated to God, with any weapons exceeding the length of one cubit' (45cm, or 18in.) – which gives us some idea of the tenor of the times!

On the Border Marches, even in towns, it would appear that qualified physicians were few and far between. For folk living in the outlying areas, medical assistance came in the form of itinerant healers and, when childbirth was imminent, women relied on the tried and tested skills of local midwives. Traditional remedies played their part and in 1574, it was reported that herbs were gathered from Hadrian's Wall to treat local people. 'The Skotts lyches or surgeons do yerely repayr to the sayd Roman Wall… to gether sundry herbes for surgery, for it is thought that the Romaynes there had planted most nedefull herbes for sundry purposes, but howsoever it was, these herbes are fownd very wholesome.' They were, however, no defence against 'plague', a word used to describe a variety of epidemics that swept through the Border country in the 16th century, some leaving a high death rate in their wake.

What little opportunity for education there was available was usually generated by the church, but in such a rough and ready society, lessons and learning were not a priority and many people were illiterate. The situation was summed up nicely by Sir John Forster who admitted 'we that inhabite Northumberland are not acquaynted with any learned or rare frazes' and in 1567, when Wat of Harden married Mary Scott, 'the Flower of Yarrow', neither Wat, his future father in law, nor their five eminent witnesses could

BELOW LEFT
This illustration of Dryhope Tower gives a good idea of the layout and living arrangements in a typical tower house. Note the entrance, which is at first-floor level and is reached via a timber fore-stair that could be swiftly dismantled in times of trouble, the spiral staircase giving access to the upper floors and the weapons and armour stored within easy reach of the defenders. (Illustration by David Simon)

BELOW
Some tower houses incorporated a kitchen within their barmkin wall and when a traveller visited Langholm in 1629, he could choose from 'mutton, midden fowle, oat bread cakes on the kirtle baked the fifth part of an inch thick; wheat bread, ale and aqua vitae'. This diet could be supplemented with beef, veal, pork, game and fish, including 'codd', 'white hearinges or red' and salmon. (The Borderers)

write their names in the marriage contract. Not everyone chose to be married in church and the tradition of 'handfasting' was an accepted form of betrothal in the Borders, whereby having 'joined hands' and passed a year of mutually agreeable cohabitation, a couple were acknowledged as partners for life. Border women were described as 'fair in complexion, comely and pleasing', and according to a Spanish ambassador, were well dressed, 'though very bold'. They took control of all domestic matters and doubtless did what they could to make life as pleasant as possible for their families. However, this was a warlike society and there is an enduring Charlton tradition whereby the lady of the house would place a spur on the headman's dish as a reminder that the larder was bare and it was time to be a' riding!

Children were valued and nurtured, but childhood could be brief. In 1593 an 11-year-old Johnstone boy had his first taste of combat at the culmination of the long-standing feud between the Maxwells and the Johnstones at the battle of Dryfe Sands near Lockerbie. No doubt during the Johnstones' relentless pursuit and slaughter of the defeated Maxwells he would have witnessed the vicious, backhanded sword swipe delivered by a passing horseman that became known as a 'Lockerbie Lick'.

The Borderer's rough sense of humour is nowhere better seen than in his bestowing of nicknames on his kinsmen, friends and enemies. Often highlighting some past incident, a physical characteristic or an unfortunate behavioural trait, these names have come down to us in Wardens' correspondence and in legal proceedings. The reason for some of them is obvious enough, whilst others we can only wonder at: Watty Wudspurs, Jock Robson the Slasher, Fingerless Will Nixon, Curst Eckie, Archie Fyre-the-Braes, Nebless Clem Croser, Davey Na' Gude Priest, Cutlugs, Wynking Will, David the Lady, Unhappy Anthone, Hob the King, Sore John, Pikehood, Halfe Drowned Georde, Andrew the Wooer, Clemmett Nyxson – the Clashe, Thom with the Lance, George Ellott called Buggerback, his brother Arche Ellott called Dogpyntle, Hob Ellott alias Bane Pryck, Bangtaile, Rob Hall alias The Porke, The Devil's Shaft Blade, Dafte Jocke, the Fryday Thief and Curst Eckie.

It was reported that Borderers put great store on their word of honour and it was said of two arch brigands that although 'they would not [hesitate] to steal… they would not betray any man that trusts in them, for all the gold in Scotland or France'. As we have seen, the Borderer would certainly put his own freedom at risk in order to rescue friends taken by the law. According to the ballad 'Jock o' the Side', when Jock was taken prisoner following a raid, three of his companions, disguised as 'country lads', rode from Liddesdale to 'Newcastle toun', broke him out of gaol and returning homeward, confounded the Land Sergeant's pursuit by daring to cross the flooded Tyne at 'Cholerford brae' 'where the water ran like mountains hie'. However, as Lord Scrope reports in 1596, honour amongst thieves did not always prevail, as when 'William Jock murdered Sim of Medop, shooting him through the head with a dagg on the moor… Sim cried out to Jock to be a good brother, as he had saved his life in the last chase they were in, but Jock shot him suddenly.'

EXPERIENCE OF BATTLE

When the Borderer was engaged in vicious, small-scale skirmishes on the Border Marches, he was invariably fighting for booty or for his family's honour and was a bold and tenacious opponent. However, his performance on the battlefield could be marred by his tenuous allegiance to the crown and in addition, such men were 'much given to the spoyl' and the lure of ransom and plunder would always take priority.

Borderers were acknowledged by both governments as fine light horsemen, and were arguably the most impressive guerrilla soldiers of their day. In times of national conflict they were conscripted into their country's armed forces as scouts, or 'prickers', and, given their activities on the Border Marches, were employed to harass the enemy's army, cut down stragglers, hinder his lines of communication, steal his livestock and, if they were part of an invading force, carry out raids on his towns and settlements. In 1544, during the 'rough wooing'. 4,000 riders from the English Marches joined the Earl of Hertford's army at Leith and were dispatched to pillage and burn the countryside around Edinburgh and are reported to have laid waste to all within a 7-mile (11km) radius of the city. They were also efficient scouts and if their country was on the receiving end of an invasion, they would shadow the advance of the enemy's forces and gather intelligence as to its strength and morale. De Beaugue reports that whilst on campaign against the English, 'my Lord Hume, a Gentleman fitted for Military Service… had gone Abroad the night before to observe the Posture and State of their [English] Army, [and] return'd with an Account of their Approach'. When they were well motivated, as many Scots were during this period of English aggression, Borderers could acquit themselves with distinction and, as the campaign progressed, de Beaugue praises their performance whilst skirmishing against the English, reporting that 'Lord Hume and the rest of our Horse did Wonders as before, broke in upon their Ranks, and carried all like a Torrent before them'.

However, national conflicts were rarely allowed to interfere with local relationships. In 1547, William Patten noted that English Borderers wore 'handkerchiefs rolled about their arms and letters broidered upon their caps', ostensibly so 'each of them might know his fellow', but suspected that by these marks, 'they might be known to the enemy as the enemy are known to them, for they have their marks too, and so, in conflict, each to spare the other'. Subsequently, on the battlefield at Pinkie Cleugh, Patten observed English 'prickers' actually conversing with their Scottish counterparts and 'when they perceived they had been spied, they began to run at one another' in a make-believe manner, 'landing few strokes but by assent and appointment'. He also notes rather shrewdly that the small badges on which the Borderers displayed their national colours were worn so lightly that 'a puff of wind might have blown them from their breasts', for should the tide of battle begin to turn against their current allies, these men were not averse to suddenly changing sides. This over-riding instinct for self-preservation – or treachery, depending on one's point of view – was to be a crucial factor in the English defeat at the battle of Ancrum Moor in 1545.

During this period of harrying in the Scottish Border Marches, Sir Ralph Eure (the grandfather of Ralph, 3rd Lord Eure), Warden of the English Middle March, and Sir Brian Laiton, Captain of Norham Castle, had earned a reputation for the excessive savagery with which they conducted their inroads into the Merse and Teviotdale. Having burnt Jedburgh and Kelso the previous year, they 'miserably plundered' the neighbouring countryside, took 800 prisoners, killed 400 others and made off with 10,000 cattle and 12,400 sheep. Eure's infamy increased when he cold-bloodedly burned the tower of Broomhouse, along with 'its lady, a noble and aged woman, her

This well-equipped raider wears a burgonet and protects his neck and shoulders with an 'Allmayne Collar'. A leather doublet, slashed hose and leather riding boots complete his costume. He is armed with a bow, a dagg and a basket-hilted sword. (The Borderers)

children and whole family'. This particular act was a cause of much outrage to the Scots, who considered it 'a deed of cruelty ill suiting Eure's courage'. The next year, Eure and Laiton, having been granted those lands they had despoiled by Henry VIII, returned to consolidate their position. Riding at the head of 3,000 mercenaries, 2,000 men of the Borders, and 700 'assured' Scots, the two commanders crossed the Border. Much of the land they were about to usurp belonged to the Earl of Angus, who had so far acted with extreme caution when dealing with these English aggressors. However, following the desecration of his ancestor's tombs at Melrose Abbey and the realization that he was about to lose everything he owned, Angus 'resolved to give them battle'. Accompanied by Governor Arran and a force of 1,500 Scots Borderers, Angus shadowed the English force as it entered Teviotdale and near the village of Ancrum, he dismounted his 'prickers'. Taking advantage of the lay of the land, he used a decoy of Scots riders to lure the pursuing English cavalry into a well-planned ambush where they ran headlong into a solid phalanx of Scottish lances. In the ensuing press, the Scots fought with 'great barbarity' and as the English force began to disintegrate, Eure's 700 'assured' Scots, sensing defeat, tore off their red crosses and turned on their English allies. Local Scots, thirsting for vengeance, joined in the fight and Eure and Laiton were slain along with 800 of their men. The remaining English were routed and 1,000 of them taken prisoner, whilst Scottish losses were reputedly in single figures. On being shown Eure's body after the battle, the victorious Arran was said to have remarked 'God have mercy on him for he was a fell cruel man.'

Whilst armies of the period were generally accompanied by small teams of physicians skilled in the treatment of battlefield injuries, medical help for many of those wounded in an encounter such as Ancrum Moor was generally confined to the skills of their companions. Given the violent nature of their activities, some Borderers doubtless had the ability to dress minor wounds, staunch bleeding or apply a rudimentary splint, but injuries that resulted in internal damage or the loss of a limb were generally beyond their skills. Given the scarcity of physicians in the Borderland, for those unfortunates who suffered serious wounds in the endless cycle of raid and reprisal, the chances of survival were slim. There is an abundance of reports by Wardens detailing

G **THE BATTLE OF FLODDEN FIELD, 1513**

Following the battle of Flodden Field, it was reported 'that certain English peasants of the neighbouring valleys went forth to plunder… and did not even spare their own countrymen'. These English Borderers were accused by the Bishop of Durham of being 'falser than the Scots and have done more harm at this tyme to our folks than the Scots did' and 'when the battle was joined, they fell to rifling and robbing as well as on our side as for the Scots, and have taken much goods besides horses and catell. And over that, they took prisoners of ours and delivered them to the Scots.' The English Borderers did well out of the whole affair, for the deserted Scottish camp was also wide open to plunder and it was reported that 'Never within the memory of man had the Scots so much wealth in their camp, for they took with them all their vessels of silver and gold' and 'had with them 4,000 feather beds; also a very great number of cannon… and innumerable wagons laden with various effects and provisions'.

Before leaving their position on Flodden Hill and marching to confront the English who had outflanked them, the Scots set fire to the rubbish from their camp. Against a backdrop of billowing smoke, these Borderers who have plundered the English camp are armed with Border 'staves' and protect themselves with a variety of helmets known as sallets, padded jacks and brigandines. Along with much booty, they have two Scottish prisoners, still in full armour, who are about to be spirited away for subsequent ransom.

In spite of James VI's efforts to stop them, men such as these continued to mount raids well into the early part of the 17th century. At the height of a feud between the Robsons and the Armstrongs, a particularly devastating raid occurred in 1611, when a heavily armed war band of Armstrongs and Elliots from Liddesdale inflicted numerous grisly injuries on a community of Robsons at Leaplish in North Tynedale. It therefore comes as no surprise to learn that law-abiding folk living close to the Borderline were still building bastle houses well into 17th century.

the grisly wounds inflicted by marauders and of folk left in the aftermath of raids with appalling injuries, being permanently crippled, disfigured, 'cruelly mangled', 'maymed' and 'hurt in peril of dethe'. Atrocities by both Scots and English were not uncommon and the dark side of the Borderer's nature is vividly illustrated in the following account of the storming and recapture of Ferniehirst Castle in 1549. It is also a good example of how a spirited assault by professional soldiers could carry the day against a well-prepared Border stronghold.

In 1547, following their defeat of the Scots at Pinkie Cleugh, the English had consolidated their victory by placing a number of garrisons in the Scottish Borders. One Scottish fortification that had remained in English hands for

some time was Ferniehirst Castle, the property of Sir John Kerr, and following the arrival of the Sieur d'Esse and his men, Kerr 'sought the assistance of the French troops to regain his ancient homestead'.

The Sieur d'Esse agreed and dispatched an advance guard of 200 French harquebusiers under the command of some of his own officers, whilst Kerr followed with his Scottish Borderers, 'the choicest of the Company'. The English garrison at Ferniehirst had a notorious reputation and their commander was described as 'one of the most Barbarous Wretches in Nature... that he had not ceas'd in committing such horrid Impieties, as would horrify the most inhumane of the Moors in Africa... during the time this Monster was in Scotland he never Ey'd a young Woman, but he Ravish'd her, nor an old one unfit to satiat his Wild Desires but he barbarously murther'd [her]'.

Advancing down the narrow path that leads toward the castle, the assault party 'discover'd twenty five English Arquebusiers, advantageously posted to dispute the Passage with them'. However, 'they were forc'd to give way upon our first attack', reports Jean de Beague. He continues, 'We drove them before us to the Gate of the Base-Court, where ten of the unablest to run were sore wounded or fell'd with Handy-blows. Yet the foremost found means to shut the Gates, and we to view their Walls from all sides.' Wasting no time, an assault party of officers and 'Gentlemen, that had come along with them', using 'some Long poles' as scaling ladders, made an assault on the wall:

> And with the Help of their Servants and the Poles, got up at last to the Top of it, not-withstanding the Stones that were thrown down, and the Arrows that were shot at them; however back'd by their Soldiers, they won the utmost [outmost] Parts of the Castle, and forc'd the Enemy to retire into a large Four-square Tower, which was in the midst of the Court. Our Arquebusiers rank'd themselves round this Tower, so that not one of those who were within, durst so much as peep out. This done some of our Men shelter'd themselves from the Enemy's Fire, by means of some Tables that were at Hand; and in a short time cut a Hole in the Wall large enough to let a Man into, or out at it... The English, thus pinn'd up and reduced to the last Extremity, lost Courage, and began to talk

The tomb of Thomas Lord Wharton, Deputy Warden of the English West March, Kirby Stephen Church, Cumbria. Without doubt, the reivers had their finest hour at the battle of Solway Moss in 1542 when on the Esk ford, a small force of Cumbrian 'prickers' under Wharton's command harried an invading Scottish army 16,000 strong causing it to flounder in the surrounding marshland, disintegrate and retreat in confusion back across the Border. (Pete Armstrong) of surrendering; accordingly the Commandant came out at the Hole our men had made, and offer'd to give up his Castle upon Condition of having his own and his Soldiers lives secur'd. To this he was answered by Orders from M. D'Esse That Servants are not to stand upon Terms with their Master.

As soon as the Commandant re-entered the tower, the attackers 'set about widening the Breach with new Vigour.' Things were in this posture when the Scots caught up with the the French under d'Esse:

Having a-lighted from, and left their Horses, as they were wont to do, [they] forced open the Gate of the Base-Court, and join'd us. The Captain could perceive this from the Dongeon, and doubted not of his hard Fate, if he should chance to fall in the Hands of the Scots, so often and so inhumanely injur'd by him; to avoid therefore present Death, he again slipt out at the Hole, and yielded himself to two French Officers. But a Scots Man, eyeing in the Person of this Tyrant, the Ravisher of his Wife and Daughters, and unable to contain his Resentment, came up ere any Body could discover his Meaning, and at one Blow struck off the Wretche's Head, so neatly, that it fell full four Paces from the Body. Above a Hundred Scots took it up on a sudden with loud Shootings rais'd it on high, and expos'd to the Eyes of all present the Punishment they had inflicted upon the Author of so many foul and villainous Actions, nay severals of them wash'd their Hands in his Blood and with as many Demonstrations of Joy, as if they had storm'd the City of London; they fix'd his Head upon a Cross of Stone, that divides three different Roads, and left it there as a Spectacle to Passengers.

In the meantime, given the 'Robberies, Massacres and Sacrileges' that the garrison had inflicted upon the Scots' friends and neighbours they could expect scant mercy. De Beaugue recounts what happened next:

Others of the Scots try'd their Skill, and contended who amongst them had the Art to cut off the Arm or Leg of an English Man with greatest Facility; and when thus they had made away with such as had fallen into their own Hands, they bought from the French: Nor lost they any time in cheapening [bargaining], but gave frankly whatever was ask'd; their very Arms they parted with for the Pleasure of charming Revenge. I remember, they purchas'd one of the Prisoners from myself for a Horse; They ty'd him Neck and Heels, laid him down in plain Field, run upon him with their Lances, Arm'd as they were, and on Horseback, kill'd him, cut his Body to Pieces and carried the divided Parcels on the sharp end of their Spears.

And so, de Beaugue concludes, the English garrison were duly repaid, 'as the saying is, in their own Coin'.

In spite of such lapses into outright barbarity, there is no doubt that these Borderers were redoubtable fighters and seemed to relish the danger and excitement of their hazardous way of life. In July 1524 Thomas, Lord Dacre recounts the following tale of a classic running skirmish on the Border Marches.

I sent my broder Sir Philppe Dacre, Knight, into Scotland, accompanied with Sir Rauff Fenwyk, Leonard Musgrave, Edward Aglyonby, and John Tempest, capteins of a parte of the King's garrisons lyeng here upon his marches, and oders of the country men being in the hole, to the numbre of M [1,000] men, who rode to their purpose, and burnt a grete towne, called Smailholme, iiij [four] myles above Kelso... and not only seased miche catall, but also wan miche bagage, and so retorned homewards. And in their said retornyng, the Scottes of Tevidale (proposing to have maid a jorney into this realme) did espie... their said home commyng. And so the said Tevidale men being... accumpanied with [local] marche men (being to geder in the hole nombre MM [2,000] men) lighted [dismounted] and lay in our menis waye. And so when our men did se the said Scottes, they in likewise lighted, and with a good and fresh courage set upon the same Scottes and put them to flighte, and thereupon lap on horsbak againe, and chaced the said Scottes, and slew about xxx (30) persons of them, and took nigh upon ccc [300], and wan thre standerdes.

However, the 'Scottes' were still a force to be reckoned with. When pursuing experienced raiders such as these Teviotdale men, the risk of an ambush was always a distinct possibility and sure enough,

A parte of the said Scottes kept themselfes to gedders, and... set upon the hinder end of our chace, and there slew John Heron the bastard and other vj [six] persons, and took the said Sir Rauf Fenwyk and Leonard Musgrave, and

Standing not far from Jedburgh, Ferniehirst Castle is a substantial tower house of the Kerrs. It has seen much alteration since its recapture by a Franco-Scottish force in 1549 and was partially rebuilt in 1598. Note the decorative panels above the principal doorway, the pepper-pot turrets and the pistol-holes positioned to cover the courtyard below.

about xx [20] persons with theim prisoners, and rescued a parte of the Scottes prisoners. Albeit thorow the Grace of God and by good fortune, our said men being in the chace (not knowing of the chace hapned behind theim until the tyme the crye rose) returned... and not only chaced the said Scottes that sett upon the hinderende of our men, but also slew and took parte of theim, and kept and wan the field clere without any further doubte, and so cam home without any more hurte or damage, which I assure your Grace was a fare fortune, seying that of trouthe, the Scottes were two for one. And fynally, for conclusion herein, our men being commen home, have clerely brought away cc [200] persons, and the Scottes had clerely away the said Sir Rauf Fenwyk and Leonard Musgrave, and about xx [20] prisoners with theim. And over this, Andrew Ker, being Wardein of the Middill Marchies of Scotland, and Marke Ker, his uncle, as sore and evill hurte, insomuche no man trusteth that they shal lyve, and many other Scottes are evill hurte... and that is the trouthe of the matier.

'Sir Rauf' was subsequently released by his captors and was back in harness soon afterwards

AFTER THE BATTLE

Once James VI of Scotland ascended the English throne in 1603, the frontier rapidly became redundant and the unique conditions that had sustained the Borderer's turbulent lifestyle suddenly ceased to exist. In order to stamp out the violence that had plagued the region for three centuries, James commenced the pacification of the Borderland, his aim to 'purgit the Borders of all the chiefest malefactors, robbers and brigands'. Draconian measures were employed from the outset and in the face of 'Jeddart Justice' (summary execution without trial), mass hangings, imprisonment, forced conscription and deportation, the heyday of the Border Reiver rapidly drew to a close.

Although most Borderers welcomed the peace and safety denied them for so long, some of the wilder spirits amongst them sailed to the Continent, selling their swords as mercenaries. In May 1607, Edward Charlton of Hesleyside in Northumberland was commissioned to select 100 men from Tynedale and Redesdale for service in Ireland and in 1620, the Scottish Privy Council decreed that 120 'rank riders' were to be dispatched to Bohemia for service in Sir Andrew Gray's regiment. Buccleuch, briefly returning from military service overseas, was particularly ruthless in clearing the reiving bands from the Borders. He is also reported to have taken 200 Liddesdale men to campaign in the Low Countries – 'the University of War' – much to the delight of King James who remarked that he was 'not altogether displeased that this rabble should be taken out of the kingdom'. Hundreds more, many of them Grahams, were forcibly relocated to the bleak moorlands of Roscommon in Ireland where they were regarded by their new neighbours as 'a fractious and naughty people'. In spite of the penalty of death that hung over any who tried to return, many apparently did so. Loyal friends sheltered some, and those of them who managed to elude capture by the 'rypers' (searchers), gradually slipped back into their old haunts. Some drifted south and worked as 'keelmen' (bargees) on Tyneside or became coal miners, at that time a profession almost as dangerous as reiving itself.

(Perhaps not surprisingly, it was some of these men who helped the Scots cross the Tyne and undermine Newcastle's city walls during the siege of 1644.)

Lawlessness lingered on in the Border country and in 1618, *A Briefe Survay and Certificate of disordered persons in South Tyne and the borders* included:

Winter's Gibbet, Redesdale, Northumberland. Even as late as 1792, vagabonds still roamed the Borderland and a certain William Winter, along with two female accomplices, robbed and 'murthered Margaret Crozier, of The Raw, a respectable old woman and seamstress'. Before long, the three culprits were duly caught and executed. Winter's body was subsequently hung in chains from a gibbet on the moorlands above Elsdon, within sight of Raw bastle where his 'heinous' crime was committed. A gibbet stands there to this day, being a stark reminder to passers-by of the region's turbulent past.

[Many] great theeves… being very infectious to their neighbours… Thomas Parker… banished into Ireland, and is returned, wee knowe not by what warrant; Launcellott Parker, his brother, much suspected emong his Neighbours; Christopher Bell, of the Peth, a common horse coper, and thought to be a greatt Conveyor of stolen horses; Hugh Nixon, of the Howsteedes, nere the Wall, reputed generally to be a theefe, and a Common Receitor of theeves and stolen goodes and one James Foster, of the Wall, who, for his infinite nomber of Fellonies, could not have escaped the hand of Justice so often as he hath done, if hee had not found extraordinary favour of some in good reputacon in the Country.

That same year, the authorities were also concerned about 'excessive drinking' and the 'greit and unnecessary number' of ale houses that were frequented by 'idill persons' who 'spend the tyme thair dyceying, cairting and uther excerceissis' and were 'the cheiff cause' of the 'disordoures and insolencies so frequentlie occurring in the same'.

And so, the Border Reiver and his turbulent world eventually faded away into the pages of folklore and history. If his life was hard and his end often marked by brutality, there must also have been exhilarating days when he found himself out on a foray, mounted on his sure-footed hobbler and cantering across the turf-covered Cheviot hills, his kinsmen by his side. And as he looked down into both kingdoms, their horizons stretching out before him, he must have experienced a freedom that is lost to us now, and, being Border-bred, it is unlikely that he would have changed his life for any other.

I ride on my fleet-footed grey,
My sword hanging doun by my knee,
My name is Little Jock Elliot,
And who daur meddle wi' me!

THE LEGACY OF THE BORDER REIVER

Traditions celebrating the days of the Border Reiver continue to flourish in the region and annual events such as the common ridings at Hawick, Selkirk, and Jedburgh are well attended by local folk and visitors alike. Many descendants of the reiving families have made their mark in the later world,

 THE GIBBET, 1648

In the 1640s, we hear the first mention of 'mosse-troupers', an evocative term applied to a small number of diehard robber bands that operated out of Liddesdale and the Debateable Land and persisted in stealing horses, rustling cattle and plundering their neighbours' property. Some may well have been restless spirits recently returned from the conflicts that raged in Europe, for there is frequent mention of Borderers who were 'brought up in the wars in Flanders and France'. As their neighbours eventually turned against them, many were destined to share the fate of this unfortunate fellow who, for his 'diverse felonies', has been 'casten and put to execution, and so jugied to hyng in an irne chayne unto suche tyme as his bones and synewes rot in sonder'.

The man to the rear is well armed and carries a brace of wheel lock pistols and a longbow wrapped against the elements. Note the close-helmet slung from his saddle. His companion, who wears a battered combed morion and a 'back and breast', puts his trust in a Border lance and a fine sword with an 'Irish' basket hilt. Note his rather shabby 'Dutch' coat. Both men carry a supply of fodder for their 'hobblers'.

Enduring traditions in the Scottish Borders celebrate the heyday of the reivers and each summer, as part of the Jedburgh Callants Festival, a large and enthusiastic cavalcade from Jedburgh, led by an elected 'Callant' (champion), gallops up to the Borderline at the Carter Bar and on reaching the 'Redeswire Stane', celebrates the affray of 1575.

amongst them Robert Burns, T. S. Eliot, Thomas Carlyle, Sir Walter Scott, Sir Alec Douglas-Home, the astronaut Neil Armstrong, the footballing Charlton brothers, Jackie Milburn, Bobby Robson, Richard Nixon, Lyndon B. Johnson, Alexander Graham Bell and Lord Armstrong, the famed Victorian industrialist and armaments manufacturer, to name but a few.

The story of the Anglo-Scottish Border Reivers was played out against a backdrop of some of the most beautiful and rugged scenery in the British Isles. Thankfully, much of the hill country where the reivers once rode remains as it was 500 years ago and for those with the necessary stamina, it is still possible to follow the 'theeves roades' that wind across the remote Cheviot Hills and to explore the narrow river valleys that twist and turn through them. Scattered across the region is an abundance of castles, tower houses, bastles and defensible churches in varying states of preservation. The Ordnance Survey map *In Search of the Border Reivers* is an invaluable guide to over 800 of these sites and for anyone who wishes to see the Border Reivers at first hand, 'The Borderers' hold regular historical re-enactments at Old Buittle Tower, near Castle Douglas in Kirkcudbrightshire. Authentically costumed and faithfully recreating Border life in the turbulent 16th century, many of them are fine horsemen and have become skilled in the use of weaponry from the period. Details of their programme of events, along with a wealth of information on the period, can be found on their website: www.theborderers.info

The living history re-enactment group 'Best of Times, Worst of Times' also give visitors the opportunity to learn more about the life and times of the Border Reiver and can be seen at various locations in the Border Marches, including The Old Gaol at Hexham, Northumberland. Built in 1332, The Old Gaol has the infamous distinction of being the first purpose-built prison in England and as one would expect, was ever busy in the 16th century. It now welcomes visitors with atmospheric audiovisual displays and numerous artefacts from the period. Opening times and further information can be accessed on the website: www.tynedaleheritage.org/Resources/GaolMain.htm

The region is served by numerous tourist information centres that are well stocked with information on the period, including details of heritage trails, festivals, museums and those castles, tower houses, bastles and defensible churches that are open to the public.

FURTHER READING

Beaugue, J. de, *The History of the Campaigns of 1548–1549* Kessinger: USA, 2009
Carey, R., *The Stirring World of Robert Carey* Constable: London, 1808
Charlton, E., *The Memorials of North Tynedale and its four surnames* J. M. Carr: Newcastle-upon-Tyne, 1870
Fraser, G. M., *The Steel Bonnets* Barrie and Jenkins: London, 1971
Marsden, J., *The Illustrated Border Ballads* Macmillan: London, 1990
Pease, H., *The Lord Wardens of the Marches* Constable: London, 1913
Ridpath, P., *Border History* Mercat Press: Edinburgh, 1979

The history attached to the Anglo-Scottish Border country draws visitors from all over the world, particularly those with riding surnames who wish to trace their ancestry. Historic sites such as Smailholm Tower, a 15th-century Pringle stronghold set amidst stunning scenery in the Tweed Valley, are popular attractions and it is not difficult to see why.

OPPOSITE
Sculpted by Thomas Clapperton, this War Memorial in Galashiels is an indication of how fondly the reiver is remembered in the Scottish Borders. With his eye fixed on the distant horizon, the rider is armed with a lance and a basket-hilted sword. For protection, he wears a burgonet, a 'back and breast' and stout leather riding boots.

INDEX

Note: numbers in **bold** refer to illustrations and maps